Julian of Norwich and the Problem of Evil

Julian of Norwich and the Problem of Evil

Richard Norton, CJN

The Lutterworth Press

THE LUTTERWORTH PRESS

P.O. Box 60
Cambridge
CB1 2NT
United Kingdom

www.lutterworth.com.
publishing@lutterworth.com

Hardback ISBN: 978 0 7188 9614 0
Paperback ISBN: 978 0 7188 9615 7
PDF ISBN: 978 0 7188 9617 1
ePub ISBN: 978 0 7188 9616 4

British Library Cataloguing in Publication Data
A record is available from the British Library

First published by The Lutterworth Press, 2023

Why did providence work in such strange and cruel ways? It was God's plan, of course. But why, he wondered, must the design be so obscure even to the most faithful?

Edward Rutherford, *London*
(London: Century Hutchinson, 1997)

For the victims and the perpetrators.

Contents

Preface

This book considers the theology of Julian of Norwich (1342-1416?) in the light of some recent debates about the Christian responses to the problem of evil and suffering. It begins by setting out some of those debates and explores the similarities and differences between those who take a largely theoretical view of the problem of evil (theodicy) and those whose interest is in providing practical pastoral care. The latter often criticise the former for being out of touch with instances of evil and suffering as lived experiences. They claim that theoretical theodicists are at best mistaken and at worst fundamentally immoral because, in the end, their understandings of evil and suffering serve to prop up and legitimise the unjust social, economic and political structures that so often bring about evil and suffering in our lives.

In exploring these claims and the robust rebuttals to them I will argue that there are three key issues for our contemporary understanding of the problem of evil. First there is the question of whether, and if so how, theoretical theodicy provides the intellectual environment and framework within which pastoral responses and activity might take place; second, the perennial problem of the nature and actions of God in relation to evil; and, third, the question of the destructive effects of evil experienced by so many people around the world every day.

The focus of this book then changes a little to a direct exploration of the theology of Julian of Norwich, its relevance and possible application to the three key issues just identified. Here I will show that Julian's theology provides practitioners and theorists alike with a rich theological context that provides much-neglected access to the problem of evil. For example, Julian's themes of God's all-embracing compassion and her images of God-as-Mother make a positive contribution in relation to human suffering. Julian's theology also helps in our approach to the three key issues in providing both eschatological hope and hope in the here and now.

Overall, In this book I argue that Julian's unique way of integrating theoretical insights with possible pastoral activity makes a positive contribution to our understandings of evil and suffering in the twenty-first century and may guard our thoughts as we seek to alleviate them.

Introduction

The chapters which follow explore how some central themes in the theology of Julian of Norwich may contribute to contemporary Christian theological debates about the problem of evil. First, it is necessary to examine some of those debates in isolation, and in doing so there is a clear focus on what is fast becoming a new point of access into the problem of evil: 'practical' or 'pastoral' theodicy. This new approach critiques traditional theoretical understandings of theodicy, and both this critique and the rebuttals offered by the theoretical theologians are considered. From here, the way lies open to provide an in-depth analysis of how the theology of Julian, though woefully neglected on either side of the debate so far, can positively contribute.

The theological consideration of the problem of evil has greatly changed from that with which many of us were familiar in the 1970s and 1980s. While the history of the problem may still be traced from the classical world, to the Fathers, Anselm and Aquinas to Leibniz and beyond, there has been a radical shift in emphasis in attempting to systematically reconcile the goodness and morality of God in the face of the existence of evil. It is no longer a subset of historical theology or the history of ideas. Rather, while acknowledging that all theodicies must to a greater or lesser degree always be theoretical, theodicy now goes further and concerns itself with how suffering individuals and groups can make sense of the evil structures that surround them and create faith-based strategies for coping with the suffering they encounter as a lived experience day by day.

This means that the theology of theodicy concerns itself far more with the moral, existential, socio-economic and political dimensions of evil, a wider context than the tracing of philosophical and theological speculations as to the origin of evil alone. In short the theology of theodicy is political theology.

To claim that the theology of theodicy is political theology is to immediately raise the three key issues with which this book is chiefly concerned: first, the theoretical context within which pastoral theodicy is possible, second the nature of God in relation to evil and suffering as a lived experience, and third that lived experience itself.

Many pastoral theodicists have, as we will see, claimed that all theoretical theodicy must be abandoned or at the very least shift its focus away from the abstract and the intellectual towards how and why people actually suffer and the effects of that suffering day by day. But this may deprive us of sufficient and robust intellectual evidence to show that theoretical theodicy is indeed as inherently immoral and irrelevant as the pastoral theodicists say that it is. Some themes found in theoretical theodicy may need to be retained in order to make sense of the pastoral position and support it. To take one rather weak example; a belief in some form of life after death may allow the believer to hope for an eventual healing of their suffering and pain and the effects of both encountered in this world. On this view suffering and affliction build our spiritual character and strengthen our souls so that we are able to sing or pray:

> *Be near me Lord Jesus, I ask thee to stay*
> *Close by me forever, and love me I pray*
> *Bless all the dear children in thy tender care*
> And fit us for heaven to live with thee there.[1]

Suffering makes souls. But paradoxically that does not provide licence for perpetuating suffering any more than repeated sinful acts bring about an increase in grace (Rom. 6:1). This 'eschatological verification' may simply put a sticking plaster over the problem, to provide the traditional opiate to produce passivity in the Church and society more generally. Some theoretical theodicists might argue that, for the time being, until death at least, it is a practical response to the problem of evil. This is a very weak argument indeed but, insofar as it is justified to use it at all, it serves to highlight that the question of the intellectual context in which pastoral theodicy is possible at all must be tackled head on.

---

1. Mrs Cecil Francis Alexander, 'Away in a Manger', a Christmas carol widely in the public domain (my emphasis added to the last line). For an insightful commentary on the relationship between this carol and theodicy see Vincent Bagan, 'Be Near Me Lord Jesus', *Dominicana*, 26 December 2013: www.donminicanajournal.org/be-near-me-lord-jesus (last accessed 4 May 2021). See also Nicholas Hartman, 'Lemon Juice and the Problem of Evil' at the same website.

The second question concerns the nature of God as it relates to human suffering. This lies at the heart of any and every theodicy. Human suffering caused by the evil acts of others and the structures of sin which produce both always stand in stark contradiction and opposition to the notions of a loving, compassionate and all-powerful God. Love and compassion represent possibilities of healing and hope and yet they are not persuasive because God seems to do nothing whatsoever to bring them about and so alleviate or eradicate the effects of suffering and its causes. God is absent. God does not care, or if he does he is unaffected by evil. Why bother to continue to believe in his love and compassion? Perhaps God in his absence and immutability is in fact not loving at all but malignant to the point of being sadistic? As flies to wanton boys are we to God, we suffer for his sport.

What may well be needed then is to engage in a discussion of what can really be known about divine love and compassion and not what we think we ought to know about them. Such an examination may cause us to think very differently about both, especially if that discussion were to revolve around God *in Christ* reconciling the world to himself. Just as the theology of theodicy is a political theology so it is also Christology, or more specifically a *theologia crucis* (= a theology of the cross of Jesus of Nazareth).

This leads to the third key issue: destructive suffering and its effects in the lives of individuals and groups. I use the term 'destructive suffering' to speak of that suffering which has such major *deleterious* effects on our personal, emotional, intellectual and spiritual lives that it attempts to delete them and often succeeds, leaving us a shadow of our former selves. Some pastoral theodicists have, as we will see, strongly argued that it is precisely for this reason that traditional theoretical theodicy is inherently immoral. It does little or nothing to address these effects and consequences. They turn instead to a *theologia crucis*, focussing on the cross of Jesus as a spiritually consolatory power for victims of affliction and atrocity. The cross of Jesus provides potential healing power if, but only if, an individual is able to identify her suffering as being borne by Jesus too, with her and for her, at Golgotha. This assumes that the victim of suffering has a Christian faith and that she believes in a mystical union of her suffering with Jesus in ways which result in an *imitatio Dei* (=imitation of God). For many people who suffer with, say, depression or a 'nervous breakdown', this is at best a pipe dream and at worst adds another layer of perplexity to their difficulties.[2]

---

2. 'Burnout's Subtle Approach', *Ministry Magazine*: www.ministrymagazine. org/archive/1996/burnouts-subtle-approach (last accessed 4 May 2021.

This book argues that the theology of Julian of Norwich provides a helpful but much neglected resource for examining all three key issues briefly outlined here. I argue that this is true even though, of course, Julian was not aware of our contemporary distinctions between theoretical and pastoral theodicy. She wrote, after all, at least 300 years before any formal formulation of the problem of evil as a specific aspect of the theological endeavour.

It is well known that Julian was an anchoress[3] who received sixteen 'showings' or 'revelations' of God in 1373 and that she wrote the 'Short Text' almost immediately afterwards and the 'Long Text' after nearly 20 years of reflection. According to my late academic colleague and friend Grace Jantzen, the Short Text 'largely restricts itself to a narration of the contents of each vision' whereas the Long Text 'adds a good deal more commentary and theological reflection and is obviously the result of much pondering'.[4] It is an 'example of theology as reflection on the experience of faith, revealing how the insights born of contemplation overflow into doctrinal teaching',[5] and includes 'many questions about the nature of God, about creation and humankind, about sin, and about the ultimate meaning and fulfilment of all things, or eschatology'.[6]

As we will see, Julian was by no means content with easy answers to the theodicic problem and nor was she satisfied with the emotional and sometimes sentimental modes of comforting which follow from them. Rather, she wanted to understand how, if at all, the notion of a loving God who had promised that 'all will be well' was compatible with the natural evil of the Black Death and the burning of the Lollard heretics of her times. In what follows I will argue that Julian posed and explored questions that have re-emerged in contemporary discussions of Christian theodicy and that her insights may make a positive contribution to those discussions. They have for too long been ignored by Julian scholars and theologians working on the problem of evil alike. In bringing Julian firmly and squarely into current debates I hope to present a new approach

---

3. For a very useful insight into the life and spirituality expected of an anchoress see Grace Jantzen, *Julian of Norwich: Mystic and Theologian* (London: SPCK, 2000), chapter 3.

4. Jantzen, *Julian of Norwich*, p. 3.

5. Joan M. Nuth, *God's Lovers in an Age of Anxiety: The Medieval English Mystics* (New York: Orbis Books, 2001), p. 100.

6. Philip Sheldrake, 'A Practical Theology of the Trinity: Julian of Norwich', in *Spirituality and Theology: Christian Living and the Doctrine of God* (Maryknoll, NY: Orbis Books, 1998), p. 101.

to the problem of evil and so extend the boundaries of the debates, if only a little.

In Chapter 1 I briefly set out why evil is problematic and has been since Epicurus.

In Chapter 2 I explore pastoral theodicy and its critiques of the theoretical approach. I then consider the main rebuttals of theoreticians to those critiques which claim:

1. that theoreticians misconceive and distort the whole problem of evil
2. that theoreticians are only interested in the problem of evil as an intellectual exercise and so wholly ignore actual instances of evil and suffering as a lived experience
3. and that 1 and 2 together demonstrate that the theoretical approach to theodicy is inherently immoral and serves only to legitimise the social, economic and political structures which so often impose suffering. In doing so, it is claimed, the theoreticians give licence and tacit intellectual support to those whom we would normally regard as evil people (the dictators in many lands being just one example).

In view of this it is of considerable importance to look at Dorothy Sölle's theology in her book *Suffering*, not least because it was her theology which laid many of the foundational arguments between the pastoralists and the theoreticians. This is considered alongside the arguments of those rigidly divided into the two camps which are as incompatible as the phenomenon of evil is supposed to be in the face of an all-loving God, through Kenneth Surin's masterly work *Theology and the Problem of Evil*.

Finally, I look at some different kinds of pastoral theodicy in order to clarify what I perceive to be a number of similarities which can be identified in their arguments.

In Chapter 3 I develop some issues in contemporary theodicy. I do so through the thought of O'Connor, Adams, Whitney and Stoeber among others, in an attempt to clarify the implications of completely abandoning the theoretical approach to the problem of evil. These discussions seem to suggest that certain theoretical contexts and themes are essential if pastoral theodicy is to be intellectually acceptable and gain traction in the academy as well as in the Church. This might be regarded as the first major issue.

The second is the traditional problem of the nature of God in relation to evil and suffering. This takes us to the very heart of all theodicy and still cries out to be resolved. I do not claim to have done so but I do attempt to clarify exactly what is meant when Christians speak of the supposed 'compassion of God'. Here I am heavily influenced by the thought of Fr Luke Penkett CJN ObJN[7] and how the theologies of Merton and Nouwen might be brought to bear on this understanding. Broadly speaking 'compassion' is taken to its linguistic roots: com-passion = alongside or with suffering. For quite obvious and basic Christian theological reasons this involves considering God's 'suffering with' as revealed in the passion, crucifixion and death of Jesus, truly a person, truly God.

As a consequence, this chapter argues that com-passion, co-suffering, suffering with is the main characteristic of God's relationship to evil and suffering. I argue that it is only suffering *with* NOT *for* that can offer even a modicum of comfort to those who suffer. Only com-passion can bring hope and healing and perhaps eventually a deeper love and commitment to God.

Then there is the question of 'destructive' suffering and here it is necessary to take some time to define its nature and its social, economic and political dimensions. The relevance of the theoretical responses of Adams, Weil, Hick and others are closely examined.

Chapters 3, 4 and 5 represent the heart of this book. Here I explore Julian's theology including her concepts of 'the Fall', sin and human nature, God's divine com-passion and the human body. To give each of these themes the proper treatment they deserve would be to write a systematic theology which might result in many volumes. This book confines itself to a brief overview of each of these themes only insofar as they relate to the matter in hand: understanding the problem of evil.

I will argue that Julian's concepts of 'the Fall' and human nature are especially important to that understanding for, as we will see, Julian provides a unique approach that strongly contrasts with the classical-medieval theodicies she inherited. It certainly has nothing whatever to do with the idea that our encounters with evil and personal suffering are somehow character building and so good for us. Far less does her theodicy have anything whatever to do with the idea that evil and suffering are punishments for so-called 'original sin' or for our own deliberate faults. I show this through a reworking of Julian's well-known concept of the Motherhood of God in Christ. My treatment of this is a departure from many other scholarly understandings of this point

---

7. Luke Penkett, *Touched by God's Spirit: How Merton, Van Gogh, Vanier and Rembrandt Influenced Henri Nouwen's Heart of Compassion*. Foreword by Rowan Williams (London: DLT, 2019).

because I want to argue that the Motherhood of God is a deliberate literary trope by which Julian places a particular emphasis on the divine com-passion in relation to evil. My treatment may also be unique because I want to draw out some of the sacramental implications of this radical divine self-giving and nurturing. I will argue that, for Julian, any discussion of divine power necessarily demands both maternal and paternal aspects.

I analyse Julian's view of the human body. Unlike much theological thinking in her own day and in the classical period she does not take a negative view of the body, nor does she condemn its many functions. To the contrary, being a body is not something to be ignored or escaped from, but rather to be embraced and treasured as the beautiful creation of God that it is – even when that body may be deformed or malfunction in some way. Julian's understanding of the human body and what bodies do is entirely positive and in this way, I argue, Julian's theology makes an equally positive contribution to our relationship to God and our contemporary Christian response to evil and bodily suffering.

I then look more closely at this positive contribution and argue that Julian's theodicy is not only extremely sensitive to our lived experience of suffering but is also rooted and grounded in the passion, death and resurrection of Jesus, all of which are compassionate.

I conclude by showing how Julian's theodicy illuminates the eschatological dimension of contemporary debates on the problem of evil in ways which provide suffering people with the resources to create a hopeful response to their plight. I also conclude that Julian speaks to both sides of the theoretical/pastoral approach to the problem of evil and when taken seriously her insights modify and perhaps eliminate the need for the hot-tempered vitriol that is cast from both sides on the other.

In short, this book shows how Julian's theological theodicy integrates both the theoretical and the pastoral dimensions in current debates in creative and innovative ways that those both in the Church and out of it have failed to notice and implement for far too long.

Chapter 1

Why the Problem of Evil is a Problem

It is a truth universally acknowledged, to misuse Jane Austen,[1] that evil and suffering exist. They affect and infect every part of our lives. This has always been so, but for people of faith, if God is good and if creation and the people in it are good because they are kept and held in the divine goodness that caused them to be, then evil and suffering pose practical, philosophical and theological problems against the very existence of God which must be answered carefully, coherently and rationally.

That the problem of evil (the theodicic problem) has so often not been answered in these ways adds to the spread of religious scepticism and avowed atheism in contemporary society. This has always been so at least from the time of classical Greece.

The philosopher Epicurus (341-270 BC) focussed on the problem of evil as a challenge to the theists of his day. He formulated a series of propositions, known as the 'Epicurean Trilemma' as follows:

> *P1. If God is willing to prevent evil but not able to do so, he is not omnipotent and therefore not God.*
>
> *P2. If God is able to prevent evil but not willing to do so, he is malevolent.*
>
> *P3. If God is both able and willing to prevent evil, how come it exists?*
>
> In sum, *if God is neither able nor willing to prevent evil, he is not good and so not God.*

---

1. Jane Austen, *Pride and Prejudice*. www.pemberley.com/janeinfo/ppv1n01.html (last accessed 16 July 2021).

The Epicurean Trilemma, developed by Leibniz and Hume, is relevant to the arguments of this book because it functions as a justification as to why we should or should not believe in God of love and justice – or indeed any god at all. Whether the Trilemma is sufficient to deny the existence of God or our faith in him, we should acknowledge the importance of Epicurus in raising concerns about evil and suffering in relation to our quest, after Anslem, for a rational and lively faith: *fides quaerens intellectum* (=faith seeking understanding).[2]

Possible Replies to the Epicurean Trilemma

1. Free Will

God wants us to love him without coercion. This means allowing for the possibility that people may not choose to do so. We have self-determination and this carries with it responsibilities. Responsibilities are especially important in our most intimate loving relationships which must always be entered into freely. Evil is an unfortunate consequence of our autonomy. If God were to intervene at any point in our wrongdoing that autonomy would be compromised. So, evil is not God's 'fault'.

It should be noted that this 'Free Will Defence' does *not* claim that God is entirely free of all responsibility for evil and suffering. If God has the power to intervene and does not then God seems to make choices. Perhaps it is in the making of choices through our autonomy that we are made in the image and likeness of God.

2. Soul Making

Our souls are incomplete. They must grow and develop by overcoming obstacles in our lives. This assumes that we have the free will to develop them or not. Evil is a necessary, though not sufficient, condition for a world in which we develop through our struggles. So God allows Evil to improve us. As we develop so we become purified and better fitted for an afterlife.

3. The Argument from Design

God designed a world that included the possibility of evil. Properly understood we would see that everything, including evil, 'works together for good'. This is a sub-set of 1 and 2 because they posit a world in which moral

---

2. G. Stanley Kane, '*Fides Quaerens Intellectum* in Anselm's Thought', *Scottish Journal of Theology*, Vol 26, issue 1 (1973), pp. 40-62.

action and growth are both possible and significant. A world designed in these ways is far better than one inhabited by God's puppets and robots.

4. Eschatological Hope

If we allow that arguments 1, 2 and 3 may have some merit then evil is finite. God will destroy it at the end of time (the *eschaton*). This offers hope that in the destruction of evil God will judge, compensate for and put into perspective all that we have suffered. The extension of this is that we must see ourselves as caught between the 'now' and the 'not-yet', a liminal space in which the promises of God are made. Moreover, the Church must be a community which looks forward in faithful hope by engaging in the corporal and spiritual acts of mercy *now*.[3]

5. God Suffers

God is not absent from evil. He stands in solidarity with us in our troubles. God weeps for Israel, Jesus suffers on the cross, the Holy Spirit grieves over our sin. They are exemplars of how we too *mutatis mutandis* might endure suffering. This response is often mistakenly regarded as a justification of why God allows evil. It is not. Rather it affirms that God is involved in the problematic nature of our sufferings and the evils we experience.

This is by no means acceptable to many Christians. It is offensive to Protestants who still insist on atonement by substitution. Others, as we will see, point to the infinite nature and impassibility of God. If God suffers, he does so on a very different level to us. Is it then still our suffering and, if so, how?

6. Theology of the Cross

Argument 5 contains the view that the suffering of God is still our suffering through the suffering of Jesus on the cross (*theologia crucis*). This is God's answer to the theodicic problem. The cross is the *only* justification of God's responsibility (if any) for the existence of evil. The work of redemption always trumps the role of Jesus' suffering. From the cross flows infinite suffering love which *is* the atonement for, judgement upon and victory over all evil.

―――――――――――――――

3. For the distinction between the corporal spiritual acts of mercy see my *How to See a Vision: Contemplative Ethics in Julian of Norwich and Teresa of Avila* (Bloomington, IN: AuthorHouse, 2013), Fn. to Preface, p. xi.

7. Fideism

According to D.Z. Phillips and other neo-Wittgensteinians who are the main proponents of fideism, theodicy does not seek to answer the problem of evil so much as to affirm basic Christian truth-claims in the face of it. God is good and in control, hence God is to be trusted despite – or even possibly because of – our suffering.

8. Protest

This position continually asks God a question: 'Why?' It objects to evil and suffering on the grounds that God *could* prevent horrendous evils, like the Holocaust, and *should* have done. Having posed and teased out possible answers, people holding this view do not turn away from God in disgust but wait. At best, this position seeks to affirm with fideism some basic Christian truths but I fear it is also fallacious, deriving an is (*could*) from an ought (*should*).

9. Rejecting Theoretical Theodicy

This view is gaining traction in the (apostate?) 'Emerging Church Movement' who oppose all systematic theoretical theology on the grounds that its terms are impenetrable to most people. This is true too, apparently, even of the language of the Eucharist, so that its celebration must be curtailed. It is not my purpose here to either describe their spurious position in detail, nor to respond to it.

As we will see, there are many respectable practical theologians who believe that theoretical approaches to theodicy are guilty of operating on a level which has little, if any practical application. Rather than work deductively from theory to praxis, if any, they work the other way around, inductively from lived experience to any general theory that might arise from it.

10. Sapiential Theodicy

This explores the outer limits of human understanding especially in relation to suffering and evil. It follows the Hebraic Wisdom tradition that recognises that God is both the giver and the taker of Wisdom. The goal is to see what can and cannot be known about evil and suffering. They are a puzzle affording infinite possibilities for a solution. The means of solving the puzzle are responding to God in love and awe.

This book is intended to demonstrate that an eleventh approach should be added to this list: mystical theodicy as we have it in *Revelations of Divine Love.* It is, I contend one of the few approaches to theodicy which can properly take account of the following additional difficulties which arise for anyone attempting to write a theodicy.

Additional Difficulties for Theodicy

1. Natural Evil

This concerns the suffering which results from volcanic explosions, earthquakes, floods, drought, plagues, diseases such as Covid 19, genetic defects and the like. Natural evil explores how, if at all, these things are compatible with the traditional predicates of God.

2. The Devil

Many Christians unwittingly practise Manichaeism. That is, they believe that there are two forces in the world engaged in a battle for supremacy: Good (God) versus Evil (Satan). The forces are for the moment equal and it is the Devil which is responsible for our suffering because he cannot accept that his final defeat has already been accomplished on the cross. Suffering and evil are the remaining skirmishes as he retreats. This is as simplistic as it is false. It is spiritually dangerous. It projects all our wrongs and responsibility for them away from ourselves and into a vague abstraction called 'The Devil'. It is a rather curious reversal of Feuerbach's psycho-theology.[4]

3. Experience

How? Why? In what ways does our suffering have anything to do with the (theoretical) issues of theodicy? What does our suffering say about our capacities for imagination and creativity? What damage has been done to us by suffering? Where is hope?

4. Horrendous Evils

What can theologians reasonably say after the Holocaust? Do we have the right to say anything in the face of sexual abuse, paedophilia, torture and genocide? If we do, what words do we use and, far more importantly,

---

4. See B.M.G. Reardon, *Religious Thought in the Nineteenth Century* (Cambridge: CUP, 1966).

dare we speak to the victims of a God of infinite goodness and love, or should we hang our heads in shame and keep a prayerful silence?

5. *Structural Sin*

Some theodicies deal with the 'innocent' suffering of individuals, taking little notice of the context(s) in which evil arises, or the ideologies, social structures and systems that comprise it. This must be included if a modern theodicy is to make sense.

6. *Metaphysics*

So now we come full circle, still asking questions. What is evil anyway? How did it begin and why? Is evil a negative thing, a privation or deviation from good? Does it have its own ontological existence, or is it no-thing so that, though real and destructive, it can only be understood in the sense that it is not-good?

In what follows we will deal with each of the responses to evil and the additional questions, especially in the debates between pastoral and theoretical theodicists to which I now turn.

Chapter 2

Pastoral versus
Theoretical Theodicy

This chapter has a special focus on the critiques of theoretical approaches to the problem of evil made by those engaged in pastoral care, Christian ministry and mission. The first section deals with many of these critiques and then summarises them in order to reveal three key areas of concern not only for the rest of the chapter but the rest of this book. They are, first, the theoretical distortions and misconceptions about the problem of evil, second, the surprising neglect of human suffering as a lived experience on the part of theoretical theodicists and, third, the immorality of the theoretical approach to theodicy.

This will lead us to the second section of this chapter, which explores some contemporary developments in the distinctions and debates between theoretical and pastoral theodicists. Although Dorothy Sölle's masterful work *Suffering* is nearly half a century old it provides one of the definitive works in modern approaches to the problem of evil. Sölle's writing and John Hick's *Evil and the God of Love* give useful critiques of the nature and structure of traditional theodicies and so remain relevant to our enquiry here. We will also explore the arguments of others, such as Kenneth Surin, who make a clear distinction between theoretical and pastoral theodicy and thus accelerate the debates between the two types of theodicy.

In the final section of this chapter we will consider various pastoral approaches to the problem of evil by examining key themes in the theologies of Sarah Pinnock, Wendy Farley, John Swinton and Jürgen Moltmann and uncover some surprising similarities in their arguments.

Critiques of Theoretical Approaches to the Problem of Evil

Traditional Theoretical Theodicy

The very word 'theodicy' is complex and asked to do so much theological 'heavy lifting' that it often wilts under the weight it is asked to carry. Tragically, undergraduates, those in ordination training and sometimes whole congregations are told that the 'theodicic problem' resolves to two simple but unanswerable conundrums: 'If God is so loving and entirely good, how come evil and suffering exist?' and 'Why do bad things happen to good people?' From the start we are told that they admit of no possible answer and everyone must just learn to live with the problem and carry on. This is as simplistic and narrow as it is dangerous. For theodicy is nothing less than the effort to comprehend the occurrence of evil within a much larger theological context and framework which forces us to reconsider everything we believe about God, the world, individual autonomy and the nature of justice. Theodicy deals with the really big questions of who we are, why we are and what we do. They cannot be passed over lightly so that we can carry on doing something else more enjoyable and less complex. Both in the lecture hall and pulpit there is a fear of asking these questions because by their very nature they are radical, going to the very core of human existence itself.

If we must have a cut-down, bite-sized version of the problem of evil we can briefly define theodicy as the defence of God and ourselves in the face of those things, both internal and external, which are inimical to human flourishing and healthy relationships with God and the world.

The term 'theodicy' first appeared as technical argot in the early eighteenth century in the writings of the philosopher G.W. Leibniz (1646-1716)[1] and especially in his book *Theodicy*. As a philosopher Leibniz regarded the problem of evil as being primarily an abstract question in the philosophy of religion, rather than a theological or practical one. For Leibniz the task of the theodicic problem was to create a semi-legal case which would place all blame away from God for the existence of evil beyond the doubt of reason. This case was intended to justify the

---

1. The edition of Leibniz's *Theodicy* used here is the translation by E.M. Huggard (London: Routledge Kegan & Paul, 1951).

ways of God to man,[2] representing through complicated analysis why God could not possibly be responsible for the evil and suffering we see around us and personally experience. This left the obvious question open and unanswered, 'If not God, what or whom?' and so leaves the lived experience of suffering largely untouched.

John Hick emphasised that this was not enough and that theodicy *must* tackle the pain and suffering experienced by so many every day. If it cannot or will not do that it is neither Christian nor biblical. He wrote: 'An implicit theodicy is at work in the Bible, at least in the sense of an effective reconciliation of profound faith in God with a deep involvement in the realities of sin and suffering',[3] and defined theodicy as 'an attempt to reconcile the unlimited goodness of an all-powerful God with the reality of Evil'.[4] From this definition Hick emphasised that the ultimate goodness of God should be consistent with the reality and experience of evil.[5]

Nick Trakakis has recently attempted to create a *via media* between Leibniz and Hick in this way: 'theodicy aims to vindicate the justice or goodness of God in the face of evil found in the world, and this it attempts to do by offering a reasonable explanation as to why God allows evil to abound in his creation'.[6]

Traditional, theoretical theodicy has always had to wrestle with the logical dilemma:

- God is good and loving
- God is omnipotent
- Yet Evil exists

and seeks to affirm divine love and omnipotence in the face of evil. This wrestling match undertaken by philosophers and philosophical theologians tries to 'prove' the compatibility between God and Evil. Their so-called 'proofs', like the historic 'proofs for the existence of God',

---

2. Milton, Paradise Lost, book 1, lines 25-26. *The Poems of John Milton*, ed. Helen Darbishire (Oxford: OUP, 1961).

3. John Hick, *Evil and the God of Love* (New York and Houndsmills: Palgrave Macmillan, 2007), P. 243.

4. John Hick, 'The Problem of Evil', in Paul Edwards (ed.). *The Encyclopedia of Philosophy* (New York: Macmillan, 1967), Vol. 3, p. 736.

5. Michael Stoeber, *Evil and the Mystics: Towards a Mystical Theodicy* (Toronto and Buffalo, NY: University of Toronto Press, 1992), p. 9.

6. Nick Trakakis, 'The Evidential Problem of Evil', in *Internet Encyclopedia of Philosophy* (31 March 2005): http://www.iep.utm.edu/evil-evi/#H4.

describe the God of the Philosophers not the God of Abraham, Isaac, Jacob and Jesus, worthy of worship and discipleship. So, as Tyron Inbody has maintained: 'In the strict sense of the term, theodicy is primarily a logical problem, a problem of how to hold apparently contradictory propositions simultaneously without contradiction.'[7]

Thus it can be said that theoretical theodicy is essentially defensive. Theoretical theodicists defend Christian belief against arguments which are contradictory and downright implausible in the face of evil. The fact that it 'usually responds to attacks pertaining to evil that are raised against religious belief by the atheologian or religious sceptic has led many to perceive theodicy as an exclusively defensive activity'.[8]

Although Stoeber admits that this 'defensive activity' is an important aspect of any effective theodicy, he regards it as negative and attempts to counter it by arguing for more positive or affirmative aspects. This begins in his understanding and definition of theodicy as 'the vindication of the beneficent care of God in the context of the existence of evil'.[9] It is on the basis of this more affirmative aspect, the beneficence of God, that he suggests that:

> An effective theodicy will involve the reconciliation of the divine attributes and evil – what can be understood in its defensive aspects. But it will also include evidence illustrating the active beneficence of the Divine, while at the same time maintaining the negative reality of evil and the obligations of social morality.[10]

In responding to the reality of evil, theoretical theodicists have proposed and explored a number of themes, some of which will be considered below, such as:

- Free Will
- Aesthetics
- Punishment and Retribution
- Teleology

---

7. Tyron Inbody, *The Transforming God: An Interpretation of Suffering and Evil* (Louisville, KY: Westminster/John Knox Press, 1997), p. 20.

8. Stoeber, *Evil and the Mystics,* p. 9.

9. Stoeber, Evil and the Mystics, p. 11.

10. Storber, *Evil and the Mystics,* p. 14.

- Eschatology
- Mystery
- Process Theodicy.[11]

It is crucial to understand each of these themes in theoretical theodicy if we are to properly evaluate the critiques raised against them by pastoral theodicists which will be examined in more detail later.

Free Will

On this view human suffering and the daily experience of evil are said to arise, at least in part, from the freely chosen actions of people where freedom is treated as the highest good that justifies the negative effects of evil actions. This Free Will Defence is often relied upon as a response to moral evil which, in turn, is said to arise from an abuse or misuse of human free will. Those supporting the Free Will Defence, such as Alvin Plantinga,[12] claim that the vast majority of pain and suffering is caused by human beings who freely choose to act against the will of God, insofar as and in the degree to which this can ever be fully known. Accordingly, 'Where sin is understood as the experience of the free choice of human beings this free will defence is perhaps the most significant theodical theme.'[13]

Punishment and Retribution

The Free Will Defence is often associated with the theme of punishment because punishment and retribution are deemed to be appropriate and proper responses to the abuse and misuse of human freedom. Punishment has enjoyed a long and unhappy history among all three of the Abrahamic faiths in which suffering is connected to the retributive justice of a wrathful God directed towards our sin and guilt. In Christianity this theme focusses on both individual sin and the concept of so-called 'original sin', which arises from a commonplace, though

---

11. This arises in Process Theology after Whitehead and Hartshorne. David Ray Griffin, *Process Theology: On Postmodernism. Morality, Pluralism, Eschatology and Demonic Evil* (Anoka, MN Process Century Press, 2017).
12. Ciro De Florio and Aldo Frigerio, 'God, Evil and Alvin Plantinga on the Free Will Defence': www.core.ac.uk/downloads/pdf/153326499.pdf (last accessed 21 April 2021).
13. Stoeber, *Evil and the Mystics,* p. 15.

flawed, interpretation of the myth of Adam and Eve.[14] As a result of their mutiny against the commands of God Adam and Eve are degraded and with them every human being ever since. The stain of the depravity of their actions has been, apparently, passed from one generation to the next through the act of sexual intercourse. Historically, at any rate, the taint of original sin has been said to be literally contained in male semen and through ejaculation and conception is, as it were, genetically transmitted, like a tendency to blonde hair or brown eyes!

In response to this primary misdeed, natural evil – the evils attendant on the environment, tornados, volcanic explosions and so on – is introduced into the world. Moral evil is directly caused by individual sin and so (naturally!) God's righteous and just punishment must punish moral evil. As we will see when we come to the critiques raised against this view by pastoral theodicists, this idea of punishment/retribution creates a Catch-22 situation: evil and suffering are considered to be either the consequence of sin or a divine retribution for sin – or quite possibly both.[15]

Those supporting this view argue that punishment is not simply 'an expression of anger or vengeance of God' but 'an act of requital demanded by a good and just God to balance out or set right a past wrong. It is a matter of justice.'[16]

Aesthetics

The aesthetic response to the problem of evil takes a 'God's eye' view of the matter and affirms that from God's perspective the universe is entirely good. It claims that the good of the whole is always greater than the sum of evil in the individual parts and that this makes a positive contribution to an overarching aesthetic ideal. That is, as Herman has argued, the beauty of the ideal justifies the negativity found in the negative parts.[17] On this view, all evil and suffering of whatsoever kind are both necessary and sufficient to maintain an aesthetic cosmic harmony and this is true even when we consider atrocities and traumas.[18] Evil then is not really a problem at all. It exists simply as a function of our narrow and limited human perspective. This is astonishing in its audaciousness, for who can

---

14. See my forthcoming *Julian of Norwich and the Doctrine of Salvation*.

15. Stoeber. *Evil and the Mystics*, p. 15.

16. Inbody, *The Transforming God*, p. 59.

17. Arthur Herman, The *Problem of Evil in Indian Thought* (Delhi: Motilal Banarsides, 1976), p. 114.

18. Inbody, *The Transforming God*, p. 42.

claim to know what an aesthetic cosmic harmony might look like, let alone know what this might mean from a divine perspective? As such this approach to theodicy is internally and fatally flawed.

Teleology

This solution suggests that a future good is justified by present evil[19] and in this way directly relates to the philosophical and theological concept of teleology: the doctrine of design or purpose in the material world. Teleology attempts an explanation of phenomena in terms of the purpose they serve rather than the cause by which they arise. In terms of the phenomenon of evil, human beings are in need of growth and improvement. Suffering and evil are necessary spurs to both because they help us develop morally and spiritually. Obstacles and struggles provoke us to greater resilience. Resilience as a quality or virtue is, according to Justine Allain-Chapman,[20] relevant in any theodicy because it is concerned with living and loving well 'through all the changing scenes of life'.[21] Stoeber argues that in teleological terms evil is 'considered a necessary component in the movement or transformation of present circumstances to some future, better, state of affairs'.[22]

The teleological approach to theodicy points out that God *allows* evil for our maturing and perfecting. As such it is pedagogic, teaching us what it is to be human at all.

Of all the recent supporters of the teleological approach to theodicy, John Hick (d. 2012) is the most well known. His theodicy is a 'soul-making', because he believed that God's purpose in creation is a positive shifting of all human beings away from our ego-centric self-centredness towards an openness to and consciousness of the ways of God. He rejected the idea of a *historical* 'Fall' from a prelapsarian state of grace, pristine moral goodness and innocence into 'original sin', preferring instead the notion of a *necessary* 'Fall' in which human beings move from a place of moral ignorance and innocence to moral and spiritual

---

19. Herman, *Problem of Evil*, p. 116.
20. Cathy Ross and Humphrey Sutton (eds.), *Bearing Witness in Hope: Christian Engagement in Challenging Times* (London: SCM Press, 2021). Allain-Chapman's contribution to this volume was reprinted in *Transforming Ministry,* Vol. 121, issue 2 (Summer 2021), pp. 29-32.
21. 'Through all the changing scenes of life / in trouble and in joy / the praises of my God shall still / my heart and tongue employ.' Tate & Brady's New Version 1696 and 1698.
22. Stoeber, *Evil and the Mystics,* p. 12.

maturity. Far from being the original disaster which is so often preached and taught, the 'Fall' is beneficial precisely because of that maturity, though Hick falls short of saying with Matthew Fox that the 'Fall' is, in fact, the original blessing.[23] Hick prefers to think of moral evil as the foreseeable outcome of the exercise of human freedom. In our original creation human beings were spiritually and morally immature but through many and various lived experiences, many of them really tough and life-threatening, we gradually develop a Christ-like character and conduct lived in freedom (Col. 1:28-29).[24] Given Hick's concept of divine love and God's omnipotent power, the evils of this world are 'justified because they will result in the fulfilment of the purpose of God in the eschaton. God will use all that happens within this environment to bring all creatures to the full vision and love of God.'[25]

This quotation leads us to a brief overview of the next theme.

Eschatology

Here evil is limited to a finite time in human history, our own and that of the world. It will end in those events which bring our individual lives and the life of the world to a close. Furthermore, the apparently irreconcilable conflict between the existence of evil and an all-powerful, all-loving God will be explained by God himself. He will, it seems, justify it as the ultimate manifestation of his loving care for us and all creatures. He will explain how, even though we neither felt nor saw it at the time, God was in fact carrying us through all the evil and suffering we encountered in his loving arms. In the meantime, we must just put up with it and try to understand that, despite all evidence to the contrary, evil and suffering will, in the end, lead us to an ever closer relationship with God which will last for eternity. As we will see when we consider the critiques of pastoral theodicists, this is not very satisfactory, promising jam tomorrow or rather an opiate to dull our sense of our suffering today. Even so, Hick argued that 'This after life redemption is understood not as a compensation for evil and suffering, but rather as a … bringing to fruition the spiritual perfection of human being.'[26]

---

23. Matthew Fox, *Original Blessing: A Primer in Creation Spirituality Presented in Four Paths, Twenty-Six Themes and Two Questions* (New York: Penguin Putnam, 1983).

24. Hick, *Evil and the God of Love,* pp. 219-35.

25. Inbody, *The Transforming God,* p. 62.

26. Barry L. Whitney, *What are they Saying about God and Evil* (Mahwah, NJ: Paulist Press, 1989), p.26.

For Hick 'soul-making' can and must continue after our death and that of the world in order to secure that ever closer relationship with God through which all evil and suffering will finally, once and for all, be overcome. This is the ultimate goal that God intended for his human creatures,[27] namely, that we actively participate in an ongoing atonement. We become co-redeemers alongside that other ultimate human co-redemptrix, the blessed Virgin Mary herself.

Mystery

This eschatological verification is shrouded in mystery. It rests on the idea that God has his own mysterious and private reasons for causing and/or permitting evil; reasons which he cannot or will not disclose until the end is near. Human beings are in no position to question that privacy or attempt to discern what those divine and private reasons might be. So we cannot assess them nor make a judgement as to whether and to what extent they might answer or resolve the problem of evil. Divine knowledge and God's secret ways[28] always 'surpass the power of human telling'.[29] This solution to the problem of evil is nothing of the kind. Evil remains untouched as the problem it is and the challenge to reasonable Christian faith that it is.

Process Theodicy

It is a sweeping generalisation to say that process theologians such as Griffin[30] tend to downplay or even deny the traditional concepts of God, but nevertheless much process theology seems to do just that, especially when it comes to the problem of evil. It struggles to explain how or why it is that God cannot or will not prevent our suffering. Indeed, they argue that the problem of evil cannot be tackled head on because traditional concepts of God and what it is to be a creature are as confused as they are rationally untenable. What is needed is first to distinguish between the traditional concepts of God, including that of total divine power, and a God who acts through persuasion alone. The God of persuasion, they argue, is far more worthy of belief, worship and commitment than the traditional God of coercive power. They further argue that the problem of evil must be deconstructed if it is to be consistent with the powers of

---

27. Hick, *Evil and the God of Love,* p. 340.
28. Inbody, *The Transforming God,* p. 64.
29. From the hymn 'Come down O Love Divine', by Bianca of Siena, tr. Richard Fredrick Littledale.
30. Griffin, *Process Theology.*

the God of persuasion. In order for this to happen, Christian theologians and individual believers must abandon any notions of divine power which imply or entail God's omnipotence, omniscience and so on. Since God allows such a substantial degree of freedom to all his creatures God chooses and allows that freedom to limit and constrain his powers. Freedom is a divinely inspired and self-imposed self-denying ordinance. So the problem of evil must remain unanswered unless or until traditional theology and the historic faith of Holy Church is dismantled in such a way that all can gather around the God of persuasion rather than any other.

Is Theoretical Theodicy Distorted?

Each of the traditional theoretical approaches to the theodicic problem we have just briefly mentioned have been subject to a number of critiques made by practical, pastoral theodicists. In *Theology and the Problem of Evil*[31] Surin argued that when the problem of evil began to emerge in its current form it did so at the hands of philosophers and so produced 'the God of the philosophers' rather than the God of Christian faith. What he called the 'project' of theodicy is fundamentally a work of solitary reflection:

> Theodicy is a philosophical and/or theological exercise involving a justification of the righteousness of God. This justification requires the theodicist to reconcile the existence of an omnipotent, omniscient and morally perfect divinity with the existence and the scale of evil. … Theodicy is a way of gathering knowledge, of justifying claims to knowledge. The theodicist's fundamental interest is in cognition, the kind of clear-headed epistemological activity that can be undertaken by the solitary contemplative subject.[32]

For Surin, then, theoretical theodicy is an essentially contemplative and epistemological activity which is highly abstract and the nature of which is discursive.[33] Within this understanding of traditional theoretical theodicy Surin has identified three key reasons as to why it is doomed to fail.

---

31. Kenneth Surin, *Theology and the Problem of Evil* (Oxford: Basil Blackwell, 1986), p. 3.
32. Surin, *Theology*, pp. 1, 21.
33. Surin, *Theology*, p. 24.

The first reason for failure is the intellectual milieu we have inherited from the Enlightenment which situates morality and Christian belief in a mechanised, secular universe. The philosophers of the Enlightenment – Locke, Berkeley, Hume, Kant and others – although in many ways different from each other had at least this in common: they removed the focus and burden of the problem of evil away from God in order to place it firmly and squarely with humankind. The entire intellectual momentum of the Enlightenment was, according to Surin, to secularise society and so transform theodicy into 'anthropodicy'.[34] Thereafter the intellectual agenda of any theodicist is 'a consequence of the penetration of rationalisation sponsored by Enlightenment thought'.[35]

In the same way John Swinton also argued that, within the cultural-historical framing of the Enlightenment, God was replaced by an increasingly anthropocentric understanding of salvation through reason and so-called human progress alone (*quod solus*). Accordingly, the problem of evil arises just as yet another conundrum to which we should bend our minds. The harder we think about the problem, the harder we apply dispassionate logic to it, the more likely it is that we will solve it and thus possess the means to eradicate evil and suffering from the world. But here God becomes a being who is 'clearly rational and orderly and whose ways are fully comprehensible and accessible through reason and logic'.[36]

Such a God, it seems to me, is a sort of divine robot. Passionless. Loveless. Not one who can love and be loved. Not a God who is likely to want to suffer the evil of torture and execution on a Roman cross. Even if we tragically and sinfully attempt to shorten the epistemological distance between creatures and the creator, God's ways can never be fully comprehensible and accessible. And even were we to do so, even were we to become God in some sense, how would we fully comprehend that these were God's ways and not something else, something of our own invention?

Surin has strongly argued that a second reason for the failure of any theoretical theodicy is that necessarily the concept of evil must be purely abstract and may itself contribute to the evil it tries to explain: 'to regard theodicy as a purely theoretical and scholarly exercise is to provide tacit sanction of the myriad evils that exist in this planet'.[37]

---

34. Surin, 'Theodicy?', *Harvard Theological Review*, Vol. 76, issue 2 (1983), pp. 227-28.
35. Surin, *Theology*, p. 44.
36. John Swinton, *Raging with Compassion: Pastoral Response to the Problem of Evil* (Grand Rapids, MI: William B. Eerdmans, 2007), pp 32-33.
37. Surin, *Theology*, p. 50.

The development of an entirely abstract, depersonalised concept of evil is one of the unavoidable implications of theoretical theodicy. It is of the very nature of theoretical theodicy to have implications that are purely theoretical.[38] So much is surely obvious, but within such a context Surin argues that a theoretical approach to theodicy is irrelevant to any and all attempts to alleviate the causes and reality of suffering as a lived experience.

Thus the third reason for the failure of theoretical theodicy lies, according to Surin, precisely in its application of reason alone. Even though the problem of evil is fundamentally beyond our ken and so confounds our hearts and minds, the goal of a purely theoretical theodicy is to make the incomprehensible explicable, a task which is, he thinks, doomed to failure from the start. He compares theoretical theodicists to the biblical Zophar, Eliphaz and Bildad – 'Job's Comforters'[39] – who in the same way sought to justify the ways of God to their afflicted friend by rationalising everything that had happened to their erstwhile friend. In the end, and despite the exercise of all their powers of intellectual persuasion, they proved to be totally useless, or as Tilley says, 'impractical':

> [Theoretical] theodicists do not respond to complaints or laments. They are not addressed to people who sin and suffer. They are addressed to abstract individual intellects which have purely theoretical problems understanding evil. Given the intellectual context, the purpose of constructing a theodicy seems purely theoretical. But in their *interminable pursuit of theory, theodicists devalue the practical issues.*[40]

According to Sarah Pinnock, like Surin and Tilley, if we define theodicy as a philosophical discourse that admits and promotes the possibility of theism (whether in defensive or explanatory mode) then living with suffering in the context of Jewish or Christian faith does not require a theoretical reconciliation between God and evil at all. For her this is especially true for theodicists working after and in the shadow of the Holocaust.[41] Rather, what is urgently demanded is a practical response

---

38. Surin, 'Theodicy?', p. 230.
39. Surin, *Theology*, pp. 52-53.
40. Terrence Tilley, *The Evils of Theodicy* (Washington, DC: Georgetown University Press, 1991), p. 229; my emphasis added.
41. Sarah Pinnock, *Beyond Theodicy: Jewish and Christian Continental Thinkers Respond to the Holocaust* (Albany, NY: SUNY Press, 2002), pp. 11 and 31.

with a clear emphasis and focus on solidarity with all who suffer, no matter who or where they may be. For Pinnock, theoretical theodicists ignore both the painful experience and the effects of evil by pushing it away from human beings and into a world of (idle) speculation, a task which is epistemologically incongruous.

Does Theoretical Theodicy Ignore Suffering?

In an article for *Perspectives in Religious Studies*, Frank L. Maudlin[42] claimed that theologians who frame the problem of evil only in abstract terms commit the 'fallacy of misplaced concreteness', which 'fails to connect their conceptual expression with the concrete matrix of Christian theism'.[43] The abstractness and apparent unreality of theoretical theodicy must be replaced by the concrete reality of the Most Holy Trinity revealing itself in human history and individual lives. The experience of atonement, redemption and salvation must be 'the key category for Christian theists in their statement and evaluation of the theoretical problem of evil'.[44] They must deal with 'the crucified God who actually suffers eternally and historically and who transforms individuals in the life-world'.[45]

For Maudlin then, the concrete concept of the Most Holy Trinity[46] – especially God in Christ reconciling the world to himself (2 Cor. 5:19) through suffering with us, for us and in us – not only utterly destroys the presumptions of theoretical theodicy to know the mind of God, but positively provides a very different access to the entire problem of evil.[47]

For many critics of theoretical theodicy, myself included, the problem of evil is essentially an existential one in its origins, applications and possible solutions. That is, evil is encountered by every human being not in theory but right here, right now and within a complex arrangement of social and economic structures (many of which may themselves be structurally sinful) that determine that individual's lived situation. It seems to follow from this, as Surin persuasively argued, that for theodicy to have any purpose and meaning whatsoever it must address specific

---

42. Frank L. Maudlin, 'Misplaced Concreteness in the Problem of Evil', *Perspectives in Religious Studies*, Vol. 11, issue 3 (Fall 1984), pp. 244-46.

43. Maudlin, 'Misplaced Concreteness', p. 246.

44. Maudlin, 'Misplaced Concreteness', p. 247.

45. Maudlin, 'Misplaced Concreteness', p. 254.

46. A concept which many may wish to argue is itself inherently theoretical and so not 'concrete' at all.

47. Maudlin, 'Misplaced Concreteness', p. 248.

evils suffered by specific individuals living in particular ways and circumstances. This, in turn, seems to call for the complete cessation of all theoretical and philosophical speculations about evil. Rather, suffering individuals require the praxis of faith: 'theodicy, then, has to engage with the sheer particularity, the radical contingency, of human evil'.[48]

Dorothy Sölle famously argued that all theology, regardless of its particular specialist area, must be concerned with reality in the world because all theology has its origin in pain. So the locus for theology is either suffering or the disregard for life we experience all the time. For Sölle, evil arises from the experience of powerlessness and weakness. Powerlessness and weakness are themselves examples of structural sin and social evil which morally and spiritually corrupt both society as a whole and particular individuals. When powerlessness and weakness are accompanied by a sense of anomie, alienation and anger occur because people find themselves cast to the margins where their voices are silenced and their autonomy is controlled by others. For Jill Graper Hernandez, the physical, emotional, psychological and social elements of this marginalisation have the dangerous propensity to result in atrocity.[49]

It is for this reason that Sölle's theology is representative of the European tradition of Political Theology. She, like Moltmann and Metz among others, shares an emphasis on the process of praxis-reflection-praxis concerning theological method and pastoral care[50] in which the only possible solution to the problem of evil is 'the abolition of circumstances in which people are forced to suffer'.[51] Sölle and Moltmann emphasise Christian praxis in empathetic solidarity with suffering people because, in their view, almost all theodicies tend to have an erroneous relationship with specific instances of evil. They lead us away from specific instances towards evil as a general phenomenon, although people who suffer only know *this* evil. Surin is very clear on this point, namely that most theodicies favour an abstract understanding of evil which cannot be mediated and is a 'social and political praxis which averts its gaze from all the cruelties that exist in the world'.[52]

---

48. Surin, *Theology*, p. 52.

49. Jill Graper Hernandez, *Early Modern Women and the Problem of Evil: Atrocity and Theodicy* (New York and Abingdon: Routledge, 2016).

50. Dorothy Sölle, *Thinking about God: An Introduction to Theology* (Philadephia: Trinity Press International, 1990), p. 71.

51. Dorothy Sölle, *Suffering*, tr. Everett R. Kahn (Philadelphia: Fortress Press, 1975), p. 2.

52. Surin, 'Theodicy?', p. 232.

Moreover, he suggests that theoretical theodicy is devoid of any positive social or political effect when it attempts to deal with the victims of extreme suffering, say the results of genocide, terrorism and all kinds of atrocity and trauma. He argues that only a praxis-orientated theodicy can begin to alleviate these kinds of suffering and even that may not be as successful as its proponents might hope, even though it locates the problem of evil in the space occupied by its victims and invariably discusses it with quite a different narrative construction in view.[53] Hernandez agrees.

Stanley Hauerwas pointed to an example of extreme evil in the case of fatal illnesses in children. These, he says, are some of the most bewildering instances of natural evil and present a most severe challenge to the Christian concept of God.[54] He cites the case of Carol Wanderhope who died of leukaemia and shows that the traditional ways of attempting to solve the problem of evil and suffering in this case simply cannot work, for here they are radically mistaken. Indeed, they are completely meaningless for;

> Even if one assumes rather physicalist accounts of 'original sin', it still does not follow that Carol Wanderhope 'deserved' leukaemia; nor does it comfort us to believe that leukaemia is the result of humankind's sinfulness and thus denotes the general disruption of God's good order. That may be, and it may help explain our general disorder, but *it does nothing to explain the particularity of Carol Wanderhope's illness.*[55]

To apply scholarly speculations to a case such as this does nothing to comfort a person living with extreme suffering and may serve only to add yet another layer of cruelty, making an already dreadful situation even worse. It does nothing to bring hope because it is not equipped or intended to do so, and in attempting to defend the goodness of God in the face of such radical suffering we develop a theology that is systematically problematic and pastorally downright dangerous.

---

53. Surin, *Theology*, p. 145.
54. Stanley Hauerwas, *Naming the Silence: God, Medicine and the Problem of Human Suffering* (Grand Rapids, MI: Williamm B. Eerdmans Publishing Co., 1990), p. 65.
55. Hauerwas, *Naming the Silence*, pp. 73-74; my emphasis added.

Is Theoretical Theodicy Inherently Immoral?

The nature of the immorality which pastoral theodicists see in theoretical theodicy may be easily stated. It generally legitimises an evil world. It specifically legitimises and supports sinful social and economic structures. In doing so it necessarily silences the voices of people who suffer. It applies general principles which are said to be universal to specific, unique and particular circumstances. Furthermore, although this could never be openly admitted, the concept of God which arises from all this is that he is either impotent to deal with evil, or he is apathetic to the problem or, worse still, he is sadistic and enjoys our suffering. I will explore how this might be so through the lens of Dorothy Sölle's theology in the next section of this chapter. For the moment, on any account the God of theoretical theodicy is entirely removed from evil and suffering in all their forms wherever they arise.

The concepts of God which underlie these views are, according to Sölle, inherently immoral because they ask us to disregard the suffering of people and look only at evil in general. They neglect the personal experience of evil to concentrate on a supposed phenomenon of evil beyond specific instances of it.[56] Her criticisms lay a firm theological foundation for the insights of pastorally minded theodicists who regard theoretical theodicy as inherently immoral. Surin, for example, appears quite angry in his remarks that theoretical theodicy always begins from a position which gives 'tacit sanction to the myriad of evils that exist on this planet'.[57]

Theoretical theodicists, he claims, do not wish to pay attention to the social and political effects of their attempts to explain evil. Tilley agrees with Surin and also criticises theoretical theodicists on the grounds, which we have already briefly encountered, that this is a deliberate deflection of our attention away from any and every action we might be motivated to make to relieve suffering.[58] For Tilley, the most obvious negative effects of theoretical theodicy are that they limit moral evil to acts conducted by individuals and ignore structural sin.[59]

Sarah Pinnock goes further and indicates that the Nazi death camps represent a radical break in human history and thought; a similar radical change in philosophical/theological methodology as it responds to evil and the structures which bring it about should necessarily follow. Tragically

---

56. Sölle, *Suffering*, p. 17.
57. Surin, *Theology*, p. 50.
58. Tilley, *Evils of Theodicy*, p. 3 and chapter 9.
59. Tilley, *Evils of Theodicy*, p. 247.

it has rarely done so and thus: 'theodicy is exposed as perpetuating moral justification of evil and rationalistic caricatures of practical faith struggles'.[60]

Pinnock sensitively reveals that camp victims and Holocaust survivors were and are disinclined to accept a theodicy that could logically reconcile the goodness of God with the evils daily meted out throughout the Third Reich.[61] According to Pinnock, it is *not* morally insensitive for victims and survivors to respond to their experience through their religious faith. What is inherently morally and theologically insensitive is when others externally impose meaning and reason on the victim's experience. To do that is to illicitly place much of the burden of responsibility on to the victims and survivors themselves. Hauerwas agrees:

> It is crucial for us to recognise that while it is perfectly appropriate for us to discover the sufferings we experience … have a telos in our service to one another in faith, it is not appropriate for us to try to force pointless suffering and pain into a teleological pattern that cannot help but be destructive. If we try to attribute these terrible results to God's secret providence, that cannot help but make God at best a tyrant and at worst a cosmic torturer.[62]

It is in this way that 'theodicy effaces the testimonies of victims. … It also sanctions the suffering of others, adopting the perspective of a dispassionate bystander.'[63]

This is, for Pinnock and others mentioned here, enough to signify the inherent immorality of theoretical theodicy. All of them concur that theoretical theodicy distorts and neglects the traditional responses of faith to evil. It reduces the importance of the experience of evil in favour of a defence of God's goodness. It is also morally dangerous because it frequently works to silence the testimony of those who suffer now or have, like Holocaust survivors, experienced some of the greatest evils imaginable. If this were not enough it also undermines the efforts of those who protest against such evils and the structures and ideologies which may produce them and so legitimises evil by ignoring its social-structural dimensions.

---

60. Pinnock, *Beyond Theodicy,* preface, p. xi.
61. Pinnock, *Beyond Theodicy,* p. 137.
62. Hauerwas, *Naming the Silence,* p. 89.
63. Pinnock, *Beyond Theodicy,* p. 188.

It is not surprising that many theoretical theodicists have strongly reacted to each of the criticisms reviewed here. Curiously and quite unexpectedly, their responses have, perhaps unwittingly, assisted in the development of a practical pastoral theodicy. But we must leave that to a later chapter.

Contemporary Distinctions and Debates

Dorothee Sölle

Dorothee Sölle's well-known book *Suffering* laid the foundations on which many pastoral approaches to the problem have been built, although nowhere does she explicitly make a radical distinction between pastoral and theoretical theodicies. This is, however, both implied and entailed in her theological methodology, which is inductive and political. As she insists elsewhere, compelling theology must always be 'a reflective description of certain experiences'.[64]

Faith and theology *must* deal only with the realities of the world as it is actually experienced, *not* as theologians or people of faith might wish it to be. It is for this reason that theodicists in both camps repeatedly return to *Suffering*. The 'certain experiences' she describes are some of the most vivid expressions of human suffering anywhere in twentieth-century theology. In fact, some of the expressions are so vivid that they have an almost cinematic detail about them because of the inclusion of her own experiences during the Nazi era, the evils of post-war capitalism and so-called 'reconstruction' in Europe, the genocide of the Vietnam war and more recent anti-feminine rhetoric which inevitably results in sexism and discrimination. For Sölle, theology is only meaningful in its ability to confront evil and suffering. For Sölle, theology is theodicy or it is nothing at all.

In order to be compelling, any theodicy *must* be primarily concerned with the social-structural and political dimensions of evil and suffering. It is, of course, precisely at this point that Sölle departs from many traditional treatments of theodicy, and indeed theology, in the Western European tradition. She does not offer a theoretical, philosophical or even systematic analysis of the problem of evil. Rather, she investigates the practical and political dimensions of the problem as a set of 'certain

---

64. Dorothee Sölle, *Christ the Representative: An Essay in Theology After the 'Death of God'*, tr. Davis Lewis (Philadelphia: Westminster Press, 1984), p. 91.

experiences' which themselves reveal the extent of complicity of social and political structures in producing and entrenching evils of many kinds.

We see this especially in chapter 3 of *Suffering,* in which Sölle describes three stages in our human reaction to our own suffering and the phenomena of evil in the world. They are not, it seems to me, unlike the Five Stages of Grief found in the Elizabeth Kubler-Ross model,[65] for after all suffering causes us to grieve. It is well known that, according to Kubler-Ross, the stages of grief include, but contrary to many popularised versions of her model, are *not* limited to:

- Denial
- Anger
- Bargaining
- Depression and
- Acceptance.

Neither does Kubler-Ross suggest, as is sometimes supposed, that these stages are strictly sequential or divided in some way from one another. They bleed into each other in ways of which the sufferer is largely unaware. Kubler-Ross does not envisage any circumstance under which a person may wake up one morning and exclaim 'Hurray! Hurray! Today I have moved from Anger to Bargaining'. Such a notion, though still peddled in the minds of much 'pop-psychology' and in the columns of agony aunts, is of course quite absurd.

It is interesting and instructive to place Sölle's three stages of our reaction to suffering:

- Hopelessness
- Lament and
- Protest

alongside the Five Stages of Grief (see Table 1).

Sölle's first stage, like that of Kubler-Ross's Denial, is a state of helplessness in which we feel and know ourselves to be powerless, isolated and alone: 'The weight of unbearable suffering makes us feel totally

---

65. Christine Gregory, 'The Five Stages of Grief: An Examination of the Kubler-Ross Model'. https://www.psycom.net/stages-of-grief (last accessed 2 February 2023).

Table 1.

Kubler-Ross	Sölle
Denial	Hopelessness and Lament
Anger	Protest
Bargaining	Lament and Protest
Depression	Hopelessness and Lament
Acceptance	Protest

helpless; we are stripped of the autonomy to think, speak, or act. We are completely controlled by the situation, and our scarcely formulated lament is more like the cry of an animal.'[66]

The second stage is one in which the 'cry of the animal' becomes a little more articulate and coherent. Biblically it is the stage of the penitential Psalms and the Book of Lamentations. By giving voice to our suffering we can, perhaps, begin to see and confront our suffering on the emotional and spiritual levels. A Christian might be well advised to use forms of interrogative prayer at this stage, though always with caution.[67]

Lament is not wholly negative. It invites us to think about how we might marshal our personal strengths and external networks of resource to overcome our suffering; 'the expression of suffering solidifies people instead of turning them in upon themselves'.[68] Lament must have practical outcomes or it is mere self-indulgence. It must lead to solidarity and organisation with one another, through which change to our circumstances might occur. These practical outcomes are: 'an indispensable step on the way to the third stage in which liberation and help for the unfortunate can be organised'.[69]

The final stage is practical. It demands organisation, solidarity and protest. It demands living with and understanding suffering people. It is not just an empathetic response but one which searches for and challenges the social-structural contexts that produce suffering. This sort of solidarity is akin to the 'preferential option for the poor' which

---

66. Sölle, *Suffering*, pp. 69-70.

67. A useful introduction to interrogative prayer can be found at https://www.prayerleader.com/longing-for-change (last accessed 7 May 2021). I say always 'with caution' because unless used sparingly it can have the unintended consequence of shortening the epistemological distance between creature and creator.

68. Sölle, *Suffering*, p. 73.

69. Sölle, *Suffering*, p. 74.

is a key feature of the liberation theologies of Latin America and parts of Africa transferred and applied to a European context. This almost inevitably ensures that her theodicy must depart from much traditional Western theodicy, which often fails to place evil in social-structural contexts.

Precisely in doing so, however, Sölle lays down the gauntlet in challenging traditional theodicies. It is a challenge which results in accusing much of the Western tradition's consideration of evil as being, at best, apathetic to the way people live and implying that this passivity leads to the worst forms of spiritual sadism and masochism. In the rest of this section it is worth teasing out exactly what it is that Sölle means by each of these apparently shocking and controversial terms.

Traditionally Western Christians have maintained that the predicates of God must include that (he) is almighty, omnipotent, all-loving and just. Sölle suggests that when we encounter the theodicic problem, large question marks must be raised against each. When we suffer, these predicates do more harm than good, for, when they are taken separately or corporately, we must come to the logical conclusion that all evil and suffering must, however distantly, emanate from God either as a test or as punishment.[70] Neither test nor punishment necessarily excludes each other and they may be particularly felt when we find ourselves hopeless and in a state of lament.

As we have already noted Hopelessness and Lament arise, for Sölle, from Powerlessness. Powerlessness is a signifier of 'the expectancy or probability held by the individual that his own behaviour cannot determine the occurrences of the outcomes or reinforcement he seeks'.[71]

Powerlessness, in this sense, is always anomic. It is always escorted by meaninglessness. If not dealt with anomie produces alienation and alienation produces affliction and affliction produces trauma. In each stage of our powerlessness we become more and more keenly aware of suffering's physical, psychological, emotional, intellectual, spiritual and social dimensions. It is the social that finally determines all the other aspects of our suffering, not just in the 'last instance', as Marx and Althusser[72] said of the economy, but throughout every stage of our experience of suffering.

---

70. Sölle, *Suffering,* p. 20.

71. Sölle, *Suffering,* p. 11.

72. Ben Brewstter, Althusser Glossary 1969, at www.marxists.org (last accessed 11 May 2021).

In this understanding of powerlessness, Sölle presents us with two strands of her concept of Christian masochism. The strands seem to entwine in an ascription of moral weakness:

> One is the vindication of divine power through human power-lessness. Affliction is regarded as human weakness that serves to demonstrate divine strength. Sickness and suffering are used for a religious purpose. ... Corresponding to this tendency is the other, on the human side to push for a willingness to suffer which is called for as a universal Christian attitude.[73]

Sölle believes that masochism is embedded here because through it all God has not stopped being all powerful; hence God must be the final source of all suffering. All suffering, then, must be borne patiently as a punishment and test. There is no option but to humbly and passively submit ourselves to it and believe that somehow (which is never made clear) we will be 'purified' by it and made more fit for the day that has no end.

Here too Sölle observes the counterpart to Christian masochism: Christian sadism. Her view seems to rest on the following propositions:

1. God is the ruler of all things, including suffering.
2. God always acts justly.
3. Therefore suffering has its origins in God and is sent by him as a punishment.

The most problematic aspect of this theology of suffering (if it can be called 'theology' at all) is, according to Sölle, that it makes divine anger the central predicate in its concept of God. The emphasis on wrath leads to a focus and emphasis on the complete and total depravity of human beings. Human beings cannot escape the ever-tightening and deadly grip of the world, the flesh and the Devil to which they are entirely given over by a God who hates all that he has made. While this view is much beloved of some forms of Protestantism and in the more extreme experimental churches, Sölle rightly argues that those who adhere to it always find themselves 'worshipping the executioner',[74] however unwittingly.

---

73. Sölle, *Suffering*, p. 17.
74. Sölle, *Suffering*, p. 28.

It is for this reason that sado-masochistic theodicies inevitably fail. It is also the key reason why so many people have come to see the Church and her teachings, especially about suffering, as entirely irrelevant to the way they live and the sufferings they encounter. In right conscience they have abandoned the Church as being at best an anachronism or, at worst, yet another agency which worsens and deepens their sufferings, however smilingly alleged concern might be expressed. For them the smiles are simply the smiles on the face of the tiger and, tragically, more often than not they are right to think that.

This failure is, according to Sölle, connected with widespread Christian and more recently secular apathy towards suffering. Apathy in this context is an inability or refusal to feel pain and this has two facets: 'denial and repression of one's own suffering and icy indifference to the suffering of others'.[75]

Apathy is the opposite of empathy and love, where empathy and love are understood as allowing ourselves to be affectionately affected. Socially and politically, apathy is the condition under which people will do almost anything to avoid suffering and are so dominated by this desire that they begin to avoid human relationships and intimate contact altogether.[76]

We have, of course, seen and experienced something very similar in personal and institutional responses to the Covid-19 pandemic. People hid their faces from one another, having condemned Islamic women for their supposed invisibility in wearing hijab, niqab and burka only a few months before the virus struck. We saw this in the shameful decision of bishops, local clergy and others to close the churches even for private prayer, to say nothing of depriving entire dioceses of the Blessed Sacrament of the Altar for more than eighteen months. Not since the Church in this country was placed under interdict during the reign of King John has such apathy to widespread suffering been shown. Even during the three waves of the Black Death during the fourteenth century and outbursts of Bubonic Plague in the Stuart period churches remained open and clergy and laity alike were actively involved in the practical alleviation of suffering, even with the distinct possibility of falling victim to these diseases themselves. What a contrast to the recent

---

75. Dorothee Sölle, *The Strength of the Weak: Towards a Christian Feminist Identity*, tr. Robert and Rita Kember (Philadelphia: Westminster Press, 1984), p. 25.
76. Sölle, *Suffering*, p.36.

situation where risk-averse clergy retreated to their rectories never to be seen again – except on the internet.

This apathy also quickly turned to anger and confrontation when at least one licensed lay reader in the Church of England had his sermon 'cancelled', 'un-platformed' and 'deleted' from the internet because he had the apparent audacity to challenge this apathy and indifference in one small market town in the West Country.

The Christian apathy of which Sölle writes, and which we have experienced since 2020, has led to a widespread cultural apathy seen in one of its most extreme forms: individualism. Ironically, of course, the apathy shown by Christians toward suffering feeds into and bolsters the very individualism which they so often and so loudly oppose. This has been so for more than a century.

Sölle writes: 'Apathy, an absence of suffering and the desire to get through life without suffering pain are all the hallmarks of the culture dominant in the First World War.'[77] Christian apathy towards suffering leads to the concept of an apathetic God. The apathetic God, Sölle argues, cannot lead us to an authentic understanding of suffering by reason of the thing it is – divine indifference. In this image of God, all human suffering is a matter of human moral, physical and emotional weakness which serves only to highlight divine strength.[78] Such an attitude fails to examine the *causes* of suffering. It neglects the suffering of others by concentrating on a demand that they simply accept it in the (often vain) hope that people will be transformed by it.

Having critiqued traditional theodicies for their sado-masochistic tendencies Sölle begins to consider theodicy as a *theologia crucis* (a theology of Christ's suffering on the cross). It is, she argues, only through the cross of Christ that human beings can establish a solidarity with the suffering of others. Human suffering is taken by Jesus Christ and presented to God as an integral part of his offering of himself to God.[79] It is here that Sölle attempts to revive the medieval ideas of suffering as an *imitatio Christi* in a contemporary context.[80] So Sölle says that:

> In the light of Auschwitz the assumption of the omnipo-
> tence of God seemed – and still seems! – to me to be a heresy,

---

77. Sölle, *Strength of the Weak,* p. 24.
78. Sölle, *Suffering,* p. 17.
79. Sölle, *Suffering,* p. 164.
80. See my *Julian of Norwich: Apostle of Pain* (Bloomington, IN: Author-house, 2020), chapter 2.

a misunderstanding of what God means. From this criticism of the theistic-patriarchal God I developed a position in which the cross of Christ stands in the centre, as an affirmation of the non-violent impotence of love in which God himself is no longer one who imposes suffering, but a fellow sufferer.[81]

God is one who not only has the ability to 'feel' pain (as in that dreadful platitude 'I feel your pain'), but to live it. The cross of Christ is the supreme expression and symbol of that. It is nothing less than a love which is directed towards the healing and welfare of all that God has made, especially human beings. It is in this way that the cross of Christ is *not* a suffering 'for' or 'on behalf of', as the doctrine of substitutionary atonement since Anselm would have it, but a suffering 'with', so that we too are empowered to suffer with and alongside those who suffer. This com-passion (suffering with) stands in stark contrast to the systematic and ecclesial apathy noted earlier.

The com-passionate divine love points Sölle in the direction of a 'mystical' approach to the theology of suffering. The theological use of the word 'mystical' is invariably slippery and so it is important to determine exactly what Sölle means by it. From the outset she is clear that she is not using the term in what is perhaps the most familiar generic term, to draw together the diverse theologies of, say, the author of *The Cloud* with that of Margery Kempe. For Sölle 'mysticism' is hardly a theological expression at all but a psychological and emotional one, in that 'mysticism' is the polar opposite of 'repression' in all its forms. Thus, 'mysticism' here is neither contemplative nor visionary but rather about being open eyed and fundamentally realistic about the nature of the world as it is. 'Every acceptance of suffering is an acceptance of that which exists.'[82]

Reality is tragic. It consists of suffering, evil and pain, all of which are inevitable because of its impermanence and uncertainty. Even our idea that things and relationships might endure can be, and often is, a cause of suffering and emotional pain. The acceptance of suffering as an acceptance of that which exists seems to imply that people will experience suffering many times during their lives. But for a reliance on the divine com-passion made known on the cross and adopted by us as *imitatio Christi*, there would be little or nothing that we could do about that. Such a position is not entirely unlike the First Noble Truth

---

81. Sölle, *Thinking about God*, pp. 187-88.
82. Sölle, *Suffering*, p. 88.

of Buddhism – dukkha – the inevitability of suffering in the samsaric circle, although there is no evidence that Sölle deliberately adopted and adapted that Noble Truth to her theology.

The denial of or apathy towards suffering is a flight from the acceptance of that which exists into sheer fantasy. Conversely, a fundamentally realistic view of the world as a place of evil and suffering supersedes and opposes every theoretical theodicy. Theodicy is replaced by a love for reality such that: 'God is the symbol of our unending capacity to love. ... Here the theme of love towards God, toward one who is certainly *not over us as a perfect being*, but one who is *in the process of becoming*, as is everything we love.'[83] David Ray Griffin and other modern 'Process' theologians might well agree.[84]

Our 'unending capacity to love' and 'the theme of love towards God' is stronger than any affliction for, traditionally at least, Christians have always believed that 'Love casts out fear' (1 John 4:18) In the light of that Johannine passage Sölle argues that 'Mystical theology answers suffering with a love in view of which "the Lord" has to feel ashamed, for it is stronger than he. But 'the Lord" is no longer the object of theology ... [for such fearless love] transcends every God who is less than love.'[85]

Sölle's approach to the problem of suffering shows her utter contempt for any theodicy which contains elements of Christian sado-masochism or apathy. In their place she provides practical help as a response to suffering through a sharing in the divine compassion, in love and solidarity with those who suffer.

As we will see later on, Sölle's theology of suffering has profoundly influenced the theodicies of Surin, Tilley, Jantzen and Pinnock to name but for. They criticise traditional theoretical theodicies even more explicitly in their 'practical/political theologies'. But first we must consider how a Theology of Hope can aid a response to the theodicic problem as proposed by Jürgen Moltmann.

Jürgen Moltmann's Theology of Hope

This section argues that 50 years or more after *Theology of Hope*, the future of theological theodicy remains a theology of what Moltmann called the dawn of the 'coming God' breaking in upon us. It is a theology which, through visions, dreams and projects, rekindles the human

---

83. Sölle, *Suffering*, p. 92; my emphasis added.
84. Griffin, *Process Theology*.
85. Sölle, *Suffering*, p. 94.

imagination to transcend the limits of reality, not in order to deny that reality but rather to extend human imagination into the sphere of the possible. It is a lack of theological, eschatological imagination that gives rise to the assessment that our current social political economic and indeed ecclesial circumstances – especially with the rise of the heresy of the Emergent Church Movement[86] – affords little or no hope.

This section challenges that assessment. It does so not because we might force ourselves to see hidden signs of hope strewn among our current problems, but because that assessment makes a category mistake between apocalyptic thinking and hope – especially Christian hope.

Whereas apocalyptic, or catastrophic, thinking involves a certain assessment of the future, hope is a theological virtue qualifying the present. To confuse the two, as I will argue, helps no one, especially not those who suffer. But to reimagine hope by reapplying some of Moltmann's themes from *Theology of Hope* to our recent experiences of natural evil through Covid-19 and the like, together with a fresh look at 1 Corinthians 13:13, might make sense of both.

Many individuals, whole congregations, approach the three Pauline virtues of faith, hope and charity (=self-giving love) from a position that tells us that they are personal, individualistic and centred on the self. As I will explain throughout this section this position is deeply flawed and results in us living a caricature of what these virtues really are. Faith, for example, becomes a counterfactual ideological position called belief which we allow ourselves to be emotionally blackmailed into holding if we want to be 'saved'. Faith, on this view, asks us to take a giant leap off the edge of a cliff, concerning the existence of God and the effect of Jesus on the world's suffering. To take that leap of faith is considered by many Christians and their leaders to be somehow meritorious, whether we have any firm conviction about these things or not.

In the same way, charity appears as a huge demand on the will. We are told that we *must* think positively and act generously towards others; and especially to those with whom we struggle and fundamentally differ, whoever they may be. We *must* do this despite or perhaps even because of our disliking and disapproval of them in almost every possible way. Once again, we *must* make this supreme self-punitive effort because it is somehow a meritorious moral and spiritual imperative.

So, hope becomes no more than a polite way of speaking about wishful thinking. We put a positive spin on the loss of any firm expectation that such and such a good thing might happen: 'Do you really think that

---

86. See my 'Emergent Church – Current Heresy', www.acadmia.edu.

you will gain such and such award?' 'No. But I live in hope.' Hope has become a mere emission of longing into a vacuum. It is what remains when there is no real expectation. But this is no more than a positive emotional spin on wishful thinking, presenting apathy, passivity and resignation in the face of evil and suffering as a virtue.

It should be obvious from these somewhat polemical paragraphs that, in my view, these three *simulacra* have little or nothing to do with the theological virtues as traditionally understood and applied to the theodicic problem.

What I propose to do throughout this section then, is to show how Christian hope, alongside the other virtues, can more clearly come to be seen for what it really is when we dare to reimagine what it is to be human and with that the evil that human beings create and inflict. I will argue that just such a reimagination is demanded by each of the virtues, but especially hope – perhaps the most important theological virtue in the alleviation of suffering.

A virtue is a stable disposition towards the good. It is generated through our habitual response to a defined set of circumstances. So, a brave person is one in whom the stable disposition of not allowing their actions to be dominated by fear when faced with danger has become a recognisable characteristic, such that it contributes to a definition of who they are. We can and do distinguish a brave person from one who simply feels no fear (because they have not properly assessed the situation). We distinguish a brave person from someone who has occasional bouts of bravado leading them to reckless behaviour. Again, a brave person is quite unlike someone who, when confronted by danger, is dominated by fear: a coward.

We learn our habitual responses through imitation. That is why virtuous role models are so important; most immediately, parents, family, peers, friends, colleagues, lovers – and even the saints of the Church! If we do not enter into rivalry or competition with our role models we will be inducted into the same stable dispositions as they have. As the philosophical works of Aristotle remind us, this is by no means an easy process. It is precarious and we need to keep a healthy distance from our models which it is not always easy to maintain. As we draw closer to each other, we find ourselves flipping from emulation to rivalry, as though the stable disposition in question, and the praise and recognition that may accompany it, were a scarce commodity which only one person can possess.

Virtue is always relational. It may begin as something external to us but it is produced and performed in us, becoming something which in some sense IS us and an objective means by which we relate to others.

If this is what we mean by 'virtue' (in general), what is a *theological* virtue? It means that the Other who produces the stable disposition in question in us is God. God is our role model. That may read as being either impossible or aspirational or both. But, as I will show, it is not. We can only think that it is aspirational and/or impossible if we begin from an individualistic view of the world where all desires start in us. Christianity never held to individualism before the second half of the nineteenth century. Even then it was profoundly reluctant to do so and only came about as the Church struggled to come to terms with scientific discoveries and the seminal works of Darwin, Marx and later Freud.

Naturally, if we start from within an individualistic consciousness, the idea of God creating virtue within us must seem somewhat magical. According to individualism, this can only come about if God directly illuminates our mind; or empowers us to a resigned waiting in the face of scarcely imaginable pie in the sky; or strengthens our will to do what we know to be right in our relationships with others, however painful, unpleasant and inappropriate that may turn out to be for us and for them. In every case what is required is for God to 'zap' us in some way. A proper understanding of the psychology in question produces both a saner and more traditional picture.

For faith is the stable disposition in us which comes about by God persuading us, through the presence of Jesus' life and death, that we are greatly loved by God just as we are, precisely because of the chaotic bits of our life – and not despite them as individualistic thinking would have us believe. Through this divine persuasion over time we are able habitually to relax into being known by God as we are with love, and to live without the fear of death. Being known by God as we are is already something in the face of which death is mute, since for God knowing someone, loving them and holding them deathlessly in being are inseparable, as Jesus both taught and demonstrated. So to the extent that we are characterised by this stable disposition of being persuaded of God's love, we are already starting to live deathlessly, being held in the knowledge that we are loved by the One for whom death *is* not.

Hence the ordinary emotional correlate of faith is relaxation. We do not have to strain belief towards something unknown. Rather, the effort, strain and hard work to conquer our suffering, which we are so regularly exhorted to both in the pulpit and out of it, is not on our part at all but on the part of the One who is trying to persuade us to relax into being known just as we are. Despite all obstacles of suffering, shame, ignorance and our inability to accept ourselves as loveable, that One is inducing in us the stable disposition of being persuaded by that One;

which persuasion for faith is itself God's gift in us. This gift is in us as a certain, empirically detectable, way of being present in the world.

Charity is the stable disposition by which God empowers us habitually to receive ourselves through, paradoxically, giving ourselves away. Once again, typically we imagine that charity involves a self-starting exercise of the will by which we *must* love God above all things and others as ourselves. The more difficult and demanding this is the better, apparently! Unless we are extremely careful and act in this way only from a sense of vocation (for example, street pastors) such a demand very quickly turns us into generous-seeming emotional blackmailers, run by all the pathologies of self-sacrifice.

Nevertheless, a sane theology – or indeed anyone who has properly understood John 4:10 – knows perfectly well that it is *because we are loved first* that we are able to love; and the presence of real love towards others in a person's life is a sure sign that they are operating out of a sense of having *being loved first.* The reason why this is important is because being loved first empowers us to receive ourselves through giving ourselves away; this is how we come to share in the life of God. For we can say that God's very being consists in giving God away. Hence the abundance of 'all that is seen and unseen', and the self-effacement of the One bringing it into being.

Charity, then, is the stable disposition by which we are gradually inducted by the crucified and risen Jesus (the human self-giving one who received himself fully through giving himself away) into sharing the inner life of God already in this life, here and now. The emotional correlate which goes along with this disposition is joy.

There is, of course, no shortage of books, pamphlets and whole academic studies concerning the theological virtues, faith and charity. This is, I suspect, because traditionally at least, each has been linked with a human faculty – intellect in the case of faith and will in the case of charity – which are always endlessly fascinating topics of conversation. Yet here I want to argue that the human faculty we should now most associate with the theological virtue of hope is neither intellect nor will, but *memory.* Memory in relation to hope is scarcely mentioned in theological texts nowadays. The standard work remains, 50 years on, Moltmann's *Theology of Hope*!

It seems important to emphasise that the theological virtue of Hope is the stable disposition by which we allow ourselves to be habitually stretched by an apparently future fullness that is dawning upon us. It is a dawn which recasts our past while forming and transforming us for who we really are and who we might, through grace, become. If the correlate of faith is relaxation and if joy is the correlate of charity, then the correlate of hope is the sense of adventure and sense of rejuvenation which accompanies it and which lies at the very heart of Christianity.

Where faith strains to hold on to what appears to be a counter-factual belief system and charity is a willed determination to do or to be good then hope can be little more than wishful thinking, and so not Christian at all. The only element in the Christian life that can matter at all is morals since that is the only thing that has any practical effect or 'bite' in our day-to-day lives. Thus, in some forms of Protestantism, the Bible becomes a rule book and the richness of Catholicism can too easily deteriorate to nothing more than a moral policeman. In both cases Christians are asked to live in a smog of impersonal moral imperatives which have almost no chance of becoming individual or collective core values. ('It says in his Word/We the Church insist that you Should, Must, Ought, Have Got (= smog) to do x or y or z.') Everything else, prayer, faith, grace, pastoral care, liturgy, the life of the Spirit, hope, earth and heaven are now too vague and insubstantial to make any difference to how we live with evil and suffering or our motivations for doing so.

I argue that this is as dangerous for the Christian life as it is nonsensical. Faith, hope and charity are not somewhat aspirational sideshows which are nice to have while the real work of learning and living properly approved behaviour goes on elsewhere. They are not something extra to morals, rather they are the three structuring dimensions of what St Paul calls 'Sonship', 'adoption as Son', or 'being turned into a Son' or, better (avoiding any gendered and discriminatory language), being an offspring of God. Faith, hope and charity are the three structuring dimensions of what it is to be an offspring, the stable dispositions by which we are inducted into being an offspring of God.

This means that there is not one compartment of our lives which contains theological virtues and another which contains ethics and moral behaviour and a third in which we encounter evil and suffering. No. Our being an offspring of God unfurls itself, deploys itself, comes to be, in our lives through each one of us being inducted into having the stable dispositions of knowing as we are known, and thus relaxing; and as these operate, of being empowered to receive ourselves by giving ourselves away and thus to share in the life of God. These stable dispositions induced in us turn us into who we really are and who we might become, and as they do so we find ourselves as one of the key *foci* of creation. In other words, these stable dispositions produced in us by God structure the operative centre from which we live out our state of being an 'offspring'. The dispositions are entirely non-directive – they do not tell us what to do or how to do it. But they do give shape to the way we work out for ourselves what to do so that what we want to do will follow from what it is that we discover ourselves to be in the process of becoming.

An essential part of being an offspring of God is to be a beneficiary of his will; what St Paul calls being an heir (Gal. 4:7). Being a beneficiary of the will of God (an heir) is also known by the dawn that is breaking upon us. It is worth spending some time teasing out what I mean here as it will help to avoid some of the major pitfalls in any discussion of a theology of hope in relation to evil and suffering, especially the tendency to regard hope as an essentially subjective matter.

Moltmann gave the lie to that when he set it in an eschatological context. But the idea persists that hope is a form of inner assurance or conviction which is quite independent of objective reality. That is entirely misleading, for the whole point of being an offspring of God and a beneficiary of his will is that our inheritance is emphatically *not* some vague hope that might or might not come upon us, rather like winning a raffle. Rather, as again Moltmann insisted, it is an entirely realistic, if essentially eschatological, expectation that is coming closer to us, just as a promise draws nearer to its fulfilment.

Moltmann wanted to emphasise this because it analogously relates to our being a beneficiary of someone's 'Will' in a legal sense, but relates directly to the most famous of all New Testament verses concerning hope: 'Now faith is the substance of things hoped for, the proof of things unseen' (Heb. 11:1). The problem with this verse, and it is one which Moltmann did not, in my view, tackle head on, is that it elides faith and hope. Furthermore, the verse reads somewhat differently depending upon whether we have something objective or subjective in view. So, for example, the RSV gives a subjective sense to both faith and hope to give 'Now faith is the *assurance* of things hoped for, the *conviction* of things unseen', as though assurance and conviction are states 'in' us. The sense I am trying to draw out is, however, something like this: 'Now, our being persuaded, yielding as it does the substance of what is hoped for, turns us into a demonstration or proof of what is unseen.' It is exactly in this way that our inheritance as offspring of God works, although it does so by analogy: At a testator's death, the promised inheritance under the will is substantially mine even though it is not yet fully in my possession. In view of that I already find myself starting to become a visible demonstration, a sign of what is on its way. Who I am is being objectively altered as someone else's promise, their desire, moves towards its fulfilment in my reception of it.

Another of the problems we have inherited from the overwhelming individualistic and mentalist accounts of the self and the life of faith in relation to the theodicic problem is that its opposite, theological virtues, are said to be produced in us directly by God without any mediation or understanding of them through other people. Thus hope, as I have already noted, is but a longing in a vacuum and the whole New Testament account of it and, I fear, Moltmann's commentary upon it become quite incomprehensible. For what is central to the New Testament account of hope is that hope was definitively opened up for us as an entirely new possibility by the action(s) of Jesus. In other words, hope is not magically conjured up in us by the intervention of a remote, removed divine other. To the contrary, we learn the virtue of hope in the same way as any other virtue – through other people.

As Moltmann made clear, it was what Jesus did on the human, anthropological, level that opened the possibility of our seeing something as available to us through the stretching examined earlier. He created it and its attractiveness by modelling the desire to achieve it, which we receive as we emulate him. This directly links with what the fourth Gospel says about Jesus being the Way, the Truth and the Life. For when it comes to Christian virtue in general and hope in particular, Jesus is the Way to be followed, the Truth to be told and the Life to be lived.

What was it then that Jesus did? First, he created the context in which his crucifixion was (and is) able to be understood as an act of supreme sacrificial Love and *not* an appeasement of the supposed wrath of God against fallen miserable sinners. He genuinely acted that out faithfully, fully and finally ('it is finished') and to its last consequences. Second, his resurrection revealed that what he had been saying and doing had been empowered by a true sense of everything that is, of all becoming: abundant self-giving life which is utterly inseparable from the life of God and his glory. In other words, his resurrection was not a *post-mortem* coda to a life well lived. It was and is the bright effervescence of reality – of what has always been the case – breaking through to disrupt the unnaturally darkened human life and culture. This irruption is brought about by an existentially authentic human being who lived and died without submission to the artificial piety of his opponents or the shadow of evil and death. In doing so he still creatively models the possibility of any and every human being receiving what he let loose in the world.

Like Moltmann, I want to emphasise what this means, what Jesus promised and what he fulfilled in us and for us by living and dying in this way. I want to emphasise that in that life and death we have access to the fullness of the deathless reality that creation truly is. The deathless reality of creation stretches out towards us and as it does so we enter a process through which we are turned into people who have the privilege of being beneficiaries of God's will and know ourselves to be his offspring. That is the Hope that is set before us and enters us, renewing who we really are through love, not condemnation. Once we understand that this is what Jesus did for us, that he was the fulfilment of God's promise from the foundation of the world, then our inheritance as beneficial offspring is already instantiated in us. In this way too we understand that hope is a fundamental part of reality. The 'new birth into a living Hope' to which 1 Peter 1:3 refers is not, and never was, a private or individual religious or moral reality. It was and remains a realignment of our whole way of being towards what reality really is, as 'what really is' begins to manifest itself in us and through us. This, it seems to me, mirrors Sölle's position if it is true that every acceptance of suffering is the acceptance of that which exists.

It is not just the case that in his living and dying and rising Jesus revealed eternal life; though that is of course true. His life, death and resurrection had content. He was shamed, degraded, cursed and silenced. His was the lot of the innocent victim then and now, for they are always cast out by the coalition of the civic and religious forces and their leadership. He occupied this space willingly and generously. This means that Jesus' presence as crucified and risen victim opens up the 'living Hope' of 1 Peter not as a neutral fact, as though he were simply revealing the existence of a previously unknown land or idea. Rather, he was opening it up in the only way in which it could be genuinely accessed by human beings: through forgiveness. Forgiveness is how the 'living Hope' realigns us with created reality, redeems the evil we do and the suffering we experience at the hands of others,

So often, too often, we hear a call from the pulpit to ask for forgiveness of sins as a moralistic device by which we can 'be saved'. But the 'living Hope' we are exploring, which realigns us with reality, does not make such a demand or impose any moral imperative at all. Rather it proclaims from the rooftops that we *are* saved. We do not become the beneficial offspring of God through any action on our part. We are beneficial offspring of God, precisely insofar and in the degree to which we recognise the new dawn breaking in upon us. Hope saves by freeing us from the false realities we create for ourselves and each other. That is what sin *is*. Sin is an ideology – a lived but false view of who and what really is. Being 'saved' is to allow ourselves to be freed from that ideology through hope which realigns us with truth.

The salvific work of hope re-members us, puts our brokenness back together making us whole. The role which memory plays in this re-membering is crucial, for memory is not something we have, it is part of what makes us the individuals we are. It is central to that which enables there to be a 'me' at all. Once again, the individualistic picture of memory is quite misleading. Memory has a collective history, providing the narrative we tell ourselves as communities, nations and even whole continents. Memory provides us with a sense of 'before' and 'after' and so of time and what might stand 'outside' or 'beyond' time – God.

The role of memory in any theodicy is important for all these reasons and because memory when combined with hope is how the narrative of God, who is outside time, comes to be lived out in our lives as a strong and stable human reality. It is how God, as it were, befriends the historical human narrative structured by time. As the kenotic passage of the Letter to the Philippians reminds us, God's narrative is of God-self as a human giving up of God-self to be a victim, even one who dies, so that each one of us may enjoy God's presence.

This self-renunciation is not simply an act of 'pardon' for a sinful past – though it is – it is also the restructuring from within of our being human. This is also another means by which we are stretched. Moltmann persuasively argued that if we allow ourselves to be stretched by memory we understand both our being human as a gift from the 'not-yet' that is coming upon us and that the stretching is salvific. It is salvific because it allows us to stand loose from the ways we have hitherto been bound into what has made us be what we are.

This means that memory is not determined by the past or any of our previous experiences of evil or suffering, Memory is the way apparent futures structure the present by narrating the past. This also means that Christian hope is not, in principle, about the future. Rather it is a quality of the *present* that is made available in our sufferings by our being stretched towards the 'not-yet' coming upon us. This seems to me to be something quite vital, life-giving. Neither the present nor the future exist as such: only the present exists. It is hope that empowers memory to enable us to live with a rich present, for that rich present is the only access we have to God.

We can illustrate this through an element in the Anglican theology of the Eucharist. The Eucharist does *not* repeat the sacrifice of the crucified Jesus. For *repeating* the sacrifice would both imply and entail that the sacrifice of Jesus was neither 'perfect' nor 'sufficient'. Rather, because the sacrifice of Jesus opened up hope for us, bringing an end to sacrifice, so the deliberately, historically opened reality of the New Creation is just there, longingly drawing us in, restructuring us from within into being 'really present' as humans consciously able to participate in a 'Real Presence' which is, in principle, quite beyond anyone.

In concluding this section I want to briefly examine the relationship between hope and patience. This is important because in the wishful-thinking model of hope, patience becomes a particularly unhelpful disposition. In the wishful-thinking model, patience is heavily disguised as a virtue whereas, in fact, it is nothing of the sort. In the wishful-thinking model of hope, patience wears a thin veneer of goodness which masks a passive-aggressive impotency in the face of a virtue. This sort of resignation can, in the end, only lead to tears, pointing us, as it does, not to hope but to despair.

Even so, if the arguments I have made here and my reflections on Moltmann's pioneering work have any merit, then the relationship between hope and patience must appear to be very different and more creative. For it is the sense of hope dawning upon us and aligning us with itself that makes it possible to face tribulations without overreacting to them. This is not to say that we do not react to them but rather that our reaction is measured, thoughtful and appropriate. The dawning hope helps us see tribulations as they are, giving us a proper perspective by which and through which to deal with them. This is another sense in which, as Moltmann famously asserted, hope comes from a situation of no hope.

Part of the wonder of that phrase is that through it there is a sense that time opens up before us. Where we have no hope we are constantly at the mercy of events and of people who create the smog in our lives which we noted earlier. Thus we are thoroughly reactive. Hope, on the other hand, allows us to take our time to do what we choose to do and thus begin to forge what we are coming to be. It is this being able to take our time, and not be panicked or persuaded into a course of action we will eventually regret, that is conducive to the emergence of the creative, technological and scientific spirit that characterises these first decades of the twenty-first century. In other words, patience, far from being a form of resignation, is the stable disposition, the true daughter of hope, of a certain hard-nosed and realistic insouciance in the face of real obstacles that are there, empowering us to creatively inhabit the present. Unlike the patience which appears in disguise there is nothing self-pitying about this at all, especially when we are confronted by the problem of evil in our own lives.

It should by now be clear why I think that the supposed link of Christian hope with an apocalyptic assessment of our current sufferings is deeply mistaken. There are many rose-tinted approaches to them. But each marks a profound and somewhat disturbing inability, or downright refusal, to face up to how difficult and dangerous we are to each other and to the world. With the recovery of a sense of Christian hope, as argued by Moltmann and as I have attempted to do here, we are able to sense that this or that expression of optimism masks a deep despair. It is only the person who is stretched by hope into a habitually patient attitude towards 'all that is seen and unseen', who is able to sit alongside hopelessness, give an accurate assessment of it and not be controlled by it.

If we are so stretched we cannot be overcome by the apparent darkness, neither are we scandalised by it but rather see it as one of the surest signs that the theological virtue of hope is indeed operative, not despite the supposed evidence to the contrary, but precisely because of it. Hope does indeed necessarily emerge from situations of no hope.

The Schism between Pastoral and Theoretical Theodicy

In his book *Theology and the Problem of Evil* Kenneth Surin approaches the theodicic problem from his belief that the essence of God is revealed on the cross of Jesus. Like Moltmann, the cross is, for him, a sign of contradiction to the traditional concept of God in theoretical theodicy. For theoretical theodicists God 'works in his mysterious ways / his wonders to perform'[87] and yet those ways are not entirely mysterious because they become both accessible and comprehensible when reason and logic are applied to them. Surin suggests that either the ways of God are mysterious in the sense of being beyond our ken, or they are not. Traditional theoretical theodicy cannot provide any practical answers to evil and suffering because it is based on two quite contradictory propositions. Theoretical theodicy is exactly that, an abstract and philosophical exercise, and we should not expect it to be applicable to the practical lived experiences of suffering and evil. It is a complete waste of time to try and adapt it to do so.[88] Surin levels this particular criticism against four traditional theodicies; the free will defence, natural law theory, process theology and evil as 'soul-making'.[89]

In response he proposes a practical/political theodicy which is essentially a *theologia crucis* in which the salvation of human beings and the redemption of their sufferings and all evil is brought about only through the life, death and resurrection of Jesus. The focus of any possible

---

87. A Christian hymn by the poet William Cowper.
88. Surin, *Theology*, p. 24.
89. Surin, *Theology*, pp. 70-105.

answers to the theodicic problem lie in God's self-revelation of himself in Jesus on the cross. The cross which Jesus bears is the self-justification of God: 'Theodicy waits on God's revelation of himself in the event of the cross of Christ.'[90] This, for Surin, is the only possible, reasonable and identifiably Christian approach to the theodicic problem. Only a *theologia crucis* can do justice to the spiritual predicaments presented by the presence of evil in the world. Surin considers theodicy to be a 'form of second-order theological discourse facilitating first-order praxis'[91] and so argues that the answers to the problem of evil lie in praxis which should be intended to overcome the cruelties and perversions that exist in our lives. It is here that it is possible to see the legacy of both Sölle and Moltmann at work in Surin's theology. He, like them, holds that the suffering of the God of Love is revealed in and through the crucifixion of Jesus. That divine suffering is useless unless and until people see that it is precisely in that divine suffering that they are empowered, equipped and enabled to be more Christ-like (*imitatio Christi*) in such a way that evil and suffering will be entirely conquered and eradicated from our midst. Only Christ-like commitment, faithful discipleship, provides the kind of practical solidarity with people who suffer that Sölle demanded.

Surin has argued that both theoretical and practical aspects must be included in any systematic theology of theodicy. They can only be distinguished from one another, he claims, by the sort of questions we pose to the problem of evil. The theoretical questions may include:

- Can evil be made intelligible?
- Is the existence of evil logically compatible with existence of an omnipotent and all-loving God?

Whereas those who take a more practical approach will ask:

- What, if any, actions does an omnipotent and all-loving God take to overcome the experience of evil and suffering of so many people?
- What, if anything, do we human beings do to overcome the experience of evil and suffering?
- To what extent, if at all, are those efforts successful?[92]

---

90. Surin, 'Theodicy?', p. 244.
91. Surin, 'Theodicy?', p. 246.
92. Surin, *Theology* pp. 59-60.

Pinnock broadly agrees with Surin here and extracts from these questions four strategic responses to evil and suffering:

> The first two issues are 'theoretical' ones concerning (1) the explanation of the origin of evil as a cosmological or anthropological question and (2) the justification of suffering, exposing God's reasons for allowing suffering.

> In contrast, evil and suffering also raise difficult 'practical' issues, namely (3) how a person can cope and even find meaning in the face of suffering and (4) how to alleviate or resist suffering by means of individual or collective action. The dominant academic approaches primarily address theoretical issues of explanation and justification.[93]

Surin and Pinnock can be said to have pioneered the contemporary distinctions between theoretical and practical theodicies and many philosophers and theologians have contributed to and extended the debate. Anastasia Foyle has usefully attempted to catalogue them.[94] The compendiums of Foyle and David Hunter make clear, in case there was any doubt, that the problem of evil is not, nor can it ever be, restricted to the logical or evidential task of reconciling concepts of God to it. Rather it is augmented and strengthened by responses to the practical problems of evil, such as how people can, and do, continue to love others and love God in the midst of horrendous atrocity and trauma.

It is to this we now turn for the remainder of this chapter.

Pastoral Responses to Suffering

Pinnock and Farley

This section concerns the theologies of Pinnock and Farley as examples of the pastoral or practical responses to evil. Both oppose traditional theodicies, finding them deficient in a number of ways. They present what may be to some minds very radical practical responses to the

---

93. Pinnock, *Beyond Theodicy*, p. 2.

94. Anastasia Foyle, 'Review of Christian Faith and the Problem of Evil', *Ars Disputandi*, Vol. 6 (2006). See also David Hunter (ed.), *The Blackwell Companion to the Problem of Evil* (Chichester: Blackwell, 2018).

problem of evil, for their task is not merely to describe suffering in relation to God, but to change it.

Pinnock enquires how it is possible to do theodicy at all after the Jewish Holocaust and goes on to confront those Jewish and Christian thinkers who argue that it is impossible to do so and that the enterprise should therefore be abandoned altogether.

Farley examines extreme evil too. She is concerned with gratuitous suffering (like the Holocaust) and the role, if any, of divine compassion within it, concluding that it is through divine compassion alone that people are able to resist evil.

In *Beyond Theodicy: Jewish and Christian Thinkers Respond to the Holocaust* Pinnock calls attention to writers who do *not* 'seek to justify the ways of God to Men'[95] by way of a traditional, theoretical approach to the problem. She includes only those thinkers who take an explicitly pastoral approach. From the Jewish tradition she uses Martin Buber and Ernst Bloch and the representatives of the Christian tradition are Gabriel Marcel and Johann Baptist Metz. In doing so Pinnock presents a number of differing theodicies but they always point towards existential and political responses to the Holocaust.

Marcel's work deals chiefly with individual 'private' suffering and demonstrates the astonishing ability which some people have to accommodate their suffering in their self-understanding, interpreting both in innovative and creative ways. Marcel is clear that private suffering is neither a test nor a divine punishment. An appeal to God cannot provide reasons for the presence of evil in the world for, like dictionary definitions of a concept, an appeal to God automatically blocks off any and every discussion thereafter. The goal of theodicy, Marcel maintains, is to create human empathy one for another but it cannot prevent suffering nor protest against it. For Marcel then, a major part of the explanation of suffering lies in the personal acceptance of it.[96]

Pinnock believes that this position is entirely passive and is therefore unacceptable. It is unacceptable too because Marcel is white, Western, middle-class and highly educated and as such Marcel is incapable of making any serious contribution to the theodicic debate, far less is he capable of saying anything useful about the Holocaust and its aftermath.[97] To be white, Western, middle-class and highly educated is the current *bête noire* of those who regard themselves as 'woke' – even, perhaps

---

95. John Milton, *Paradise Lost,* book 1, line 25.
96. Pinnock, *Beyond Theodicy,* p. 33.
97. Pinnock, *Beyond Theodicy,* p. 36.

especially, in university departments in many disciplines. In the specific case of theodicy, this academic orthodoxy regards those like Marcel as anathema because they (allegedly) always de-humanise victims and so cannot provide 'postures of availability which enable meaning making'.[98]

For Pinnock, Marcel's position *may* be appropriate in some limited situations, but only in the most private of them. It can never be applied more generally and certainly not to genocides such as the Holocaust. I think that here Pinnock shows a degree either of misunderstanding of Marcel's position or theological naivety, since Marcel is clear from the outset, as we have noted, that his work is *not* concerned with the bigger picture but only with the individual and private.

Buber, conversely, situates individual responses to suffering in the dynamics of his well-known construction of an I-Thou relationship with God and other people. The I-Thou relationship sustains religious faith and gives meaning and purpose to the lives of those who suffer. Furthermore, the I-Thou relationships are active rather than passive. They invite individuals to take some personal responsibility for their reaction to suffering and, moreover, to engage in interpersonal relationships and community building to alleviate it.

Although another white, Western, middle-class and highly educated male, Buber is, Pinnock maintains, much better placed than Marcel to impose notions of individual suffering on to major international incidents of suffering such as the Holocaust. According to Pinnock, Buber's advantage is that he neither defends God's goodness with reasons as to why God might permit evil, nor does he comment on whether or not God has the power and will to prevent or eliminate evil. (But neither did Marcel!) Rather, according to Pinnock, Buber recommends practising 'prophetic' prayer[99] that questions God, and this is the most fitting faith response to evil.[100]

For Buber, prophetic prayer is the highest form of expression of the ancient prophetic aspect of the faith of Judaism. It is through the Jewish prophecy and the prayer that arises from it that people are encouraged to engage in moral acts and protest. These three, prophetic prayer, moral acts and protest are the tools through which communities can be built and relationships healed.[101] Thus, for Buber, human 'suffering can be

---

98. Pinnock, *Beyond Theodicy*, p. 37.

99. For the more recent developments in 'prophetic' prayer and its use in religious groups see www.jfoutreach.org (last accessed 17 May 2021).

100. Pinnock, *Beyond Theodicy*, p. 48.

101. Pinnock, *Beyond Theodicy*, pp. 50-51.

interpreted as part of the redemption process, consisting of the mending of human relationships and the reuniting of God and the world'.[102]

Nevertheless, Pinnock disputes Buber's 'fundamental level of coping and responding to socially caused suffering' precisely because it is interpersonal. So she claims that Buber's 'view of religious hope lacks eschatological urgency and expectancy that demand revolutionary social change' and his 'communal faith response to suffering does not articulate the importance of collective political action to resist the conditions causing suffering'.[103] Thus far, Pinnock brings us to a very sorry state of affairs indeed. She condemns Marcel's position for being too individual and passive. It is not sufficiently communal. At the same time Buber's position, though communal, is not, apparently, communal enough and since his idea of community building begins with individual prayer and response it too must be largely rejected. Pinnock cannot have it both ways. Either our response to suffering is individual and private or it is collective or communal. A proper response may well be a combination of both, but after that there is simply nothing else to be had. Apart from a return to theoretical theodicy, which Pinnock also rejects, no other responses are available.

Both Bloch and Metz were influenced by Marxist theory and so they emphasise the political and social dimensions of evil to a much greater extent than either Marcel or Buber. Pinnock says that the concept of hope in the writings of Ernst Bloch (which later influenced Moltmann's *theologia crucis*) is 'a political model of religious faith involving revolutionary political activity, which accompanies anticipation of the ultimate future ... [And so] the practices of hope are criticisms of ideologies and oppressive conditions, and political resistance.'[104]

It is difficult to see how an ultimate future might be 'anticipated'. Perhaps Pinnock means the 'expectation' of an ultimate future. If so, this would be rather more consistent with the legacy of Bloch's thought in the writings of Jürgen Moltmann; see especially in *The Crucified God*,[105] for it is in this book that Moltmann sets out how the cross of Christ provides an exemplar for coping with suffering and a way out of it (=redemption).[106]

---

102. Pinnock, *Beyond Theodicy*, p. 49.
103. Pinnock, *Beyond Theodicy*, p. 54.
104. Pinnock, *Beyond Theodicy*, pp. 69-70.
105. Jürgen Moltmann, *The Crucified God*, tr. R.A. Wilson and John Bowden (London: SPCK, 1974).
106. Pinnock, *Beyond Theodicy*, pp. 88-90.

Metz was also influenced by Bloch's concept of hope and, like him, concludes that collective protest is an appropriate Christian response to suffering. Indeed, it may be the only appropriate response. Metz does not believe that traditional Christian doctrines are particularly useful in formulating a systematic but practical theodicy. He singles out the traditional doctrine of the Most Holy. It is the most abstract of all Christian doctrines, necessarily demanding a series of speculations about the inner life of God which are far removed from human time and experience.[107] The same is true of some notions in the doctrine of atonement.[108] For Metz, the death of Christ is neither inevitable nor pre-ordained. It is not a vicarious sacrifice either. It is a suffering 'with', not 'for' or 'on behalf of'. Christ's death must be freely chosen, or it is meaningless in the lives of people. If it is not freely chosen, if Christ's suffering is not a demonstration of God's solidarity with our suffering, it cannot offer redemption, for God could not understand our suffering. Only if this is the case can the stories about Christ's death, as in the Gospels, become a rich 'source of hope as well as critical memory'.[109]

For Metz, to be human is to suffer. This cannot be ignored for it motivates and compels us to 'analyse the causes of suffering, a step necessary for developing political strategies for resistance'.[110] Suffering prompts resistance and resistance prompts social change. For Metz, no good can come from 'suffering in silence' as the saying goes. Suffering has a purpose and goal which is nothing less than to change the world. This can come about if, but only if, people join together to protest against and eliminate any and every unjust state of affairs, any and every incidence of structural sin and so create a better way of human living. The only effective response to evil and suffering in our lives is collective (political) action.

Pinnock's own theodicy is an inter-disciplinary fusion of the philosophy of religion, post-Holocaust thought and political theology without being entirely eclectic. Together these elements provide her with a dynamic vision based on religious hope and political action. She makes a large number of insightful and nuanced judgements, especially as to

---

107. Manuel Losada-Sierra and John Mandalios, *A Time for the Marginal: Levinas and Metz on Biblical Time* (Griffiths University, Australia): www. core.ac.uk/download/pdf/143864383.pdf (last accessed 18 May 2021).
108. See my *Julian of Norwich and the Doctrine of Salvation*.
109. Pinnock, *Beyond Theodicy*, p. 88.
110. Pinnock, *Beyond Theodicy*, p. 91.

whether the existential is to be preferred over the political or vice versa. She is conflicted on this point without, I think, concluding that elements of both employed at the same time might be demanded by the theodicy she seeks.

Pinnock's overwhelming desire is to demonstrate beyond doubt that all theoretical theodicies are as futile as they are harmful in the practical need to cope with and confront our suffering. She provides persuasive arguments as to why they must be rejected. But she also dismisses the four writers, Marcel, Buber, Bloch and Metz which she has previously invoked to support her position. It appears that they too must be rejected because, like theoretical theodicists, they perpetuate the scandal of inherent immorality which, she thinks, lies at the core of every theodicy, whether theoretical or practical.

Pinnock argues that understanding suffering within the context of religious faith *never* requires an attempt to reconcile God and Evil.[111] Our response to evil and suffering does not ever require an abstract, intellectual or systematic underpinning. The only thing that matters is a personal and communal political solidarity with people who suffer.[112] She concludes that pastoral approaches to theodicy are always preferable to theoretical ones since they have the supreme advantage of being tested in 'real-life' situations and specific social contexts – even if they lack theological or logical coherence!

In her book *Tragic Vision and Divine Compassion: A Contemporary Theodicy,*[113] Wendy Farley departs from theoretical theodicies in three main ways:

- Her focus is on 'radical suffering' not sin;
- She takes tragedy, not the so-called 'original sin' of Adam and Eve, as being pivotal for theodicy; and
- She rejects hegemony and domination as a proper understanding of the dynamics of power.

Hence, 'One of the most terrible beliefs of Christianity is that God punishes us with suffering.'[114] This belief, she maintains, serves to justify the suffering of grief-stricken people and those who suffer all kinds of

---

111. Pinnock, *Beyond Theodicy,* p. 11.
112. Pinnock, *Beyond Theodicy,* p. 131.
113. Wendy Farley, *Tragic Vision and Divine Compassion: A Contemporary Theodicy* (Louisville, KY: Westminster/John Knox Press, 1990).
114. Farley, *Tragic Vision,* p. 118.

pain. It justifies their continued suffering as a 'good thing' and endorses the structures or incidents that brought it about. She argues that this 'theology conspires with pain to lock God away from the sufferer, for whom God becomes the ostensibly righteous torturer. The love of God is gone, and the pious sufferer is betrayed into the hands of despair.'[115]

To correct this theological error, Farley moves rapidly away from those theoretical theodicies that are based on cosmic guilt, punishment and the idea, much beloved by Protestants, that the atonement of Christ somehow appeases the wrath of God. In its place she writes of a tragic vision and compassionate defiance.[116] The tragic vision of her title is derived from two sources; the classical Greek tragedies in which suffering is regarded as inevitable and the biblical, prophetic, voices raised against injustice. Her underlying premise is, I think, that evil and suffering are inescapable parts of what it is to live in the world as it is and has always been and that our human freedom is 'the tragic flaw in human existence, at once the stamp of its greatness and its destruction'.[117] Furthermore, 'a tragic vision is concerned with the resistance to evil rather than a justification of evil'.[118]

Farley's tragic vision critiques traditional approaches to the problem of evil because of their concentration on sin, retributive punishment and an understanding of the doctrine of the atonement as an offering to divert divine wrath. In doing so, Farley's basic position is not unlike that of Sölle in that 'radical suffering'[119] – the undeserved suffering that dehumanises and destroys people – defies explanation through traditional categories and so these categories are largely redundant and meaningless in any attempt to provide a new or reconstructed theodicy with a pastoral focus: 'radical suffering confronts theology with a problem that cannot be addressed within the contest of the myth of the Fall',[120] because theological theodicy is dominated by 'the thematics of guilt' and hence, 'do not have the tools to recognise or respond to the existence of unjust and destructive suffering'.[121]

Farley offers a very different paradigm in which radical suffering and evil are handled in ways that cannot connect them to sin, guilt or divine

---

115. Farley, *Tragic Vision*, p. 119.
116. Farley, *Tragic Vision*, p. 29.
117. Farley, *Tragic Vision*, p. 37.
118. Farley, *Tragic Vision*, p. 97.
119. Farley, *Tragic Vision*, pp. 51-59.
120. Farley, *Tragic Vision*, p. 29.
121. Farley, *Tragic Vision*, p. 29.

wrath. Certainly, theodicy must have nothing to do with atonement theories. It is immoral to explain the existence of suffering and evil in relation to any form of punishment – 'penal theodicy'.[122] She argues that none of the traditional theodicies can hold in the face of radical suffering. Indeed, they flee from it in their inadequacy and failures. What is required, according to Farley, is a pastoral theodicy based on a phenomenology of com-passion[123] which speaks of God's all-embracing love, not anger.

Human beings experience this love of God through divine compassion which empowers people to actively resist evil and suffering. For Farley, God is neither indifferent nor powerless before evil. Rather, God is present and active through divine com-passion. Divine com-passion is a power or force (Spirit?) but not one that conquers, dominates or eradicates evil. Divine com-passion is entirely non-coercive, allowing for the possibility of evil in the world and in our lives but, at the same time, resists that evil – even, perhaps especially, when we are least aware of it.[124]

Swinton

John Swinton[125] argues for a pastoral theodicy embedded in the life of the Church which refuses to explain evil, but instead presents ways in which evil and suffering can be resisted and transformed.[126] He attempts to deconstruct traditional theodicies in order to help lay Christians develop and perform their pastoral care ever more faithfully. Theodicy is a function of faithful discipleship. This is made clear in his definition of what, for him, practical/pastoral theodicy is:

> Practical theodicy is a process wherein the Church community, in and through its practices, offers ... subversive modes of resistance to the evil and suffering experienced by the world. The goal of practical theodicy is, by practising these gestures of redemption, to enable people to continue to love God in the face of evil and suffering and in so doing to prevent tragic suffering from becoming evil.[127]

---

122. Farley, Tragic Vision, p. 21.
123. Farley, *Tragic Vision*, p. 70.
124. Farley, *Tragic Vision*, pp. 97-101.
125. Swinton, *Raging with Compassion*.
126. Swinton, *Raging with Compassion*, p. 4.
127. Swinton, *Raging with Compassion*, p. 85.

Swinton prevents this from becoming a sort of Christian stoicism, or the sado-masochism we noted earlier, by insisting that the Christian resistance to evil and suffering can only come about when a community of faith deliberately recovers and applies the biblical themes of lament, mutual forgiveness, thoughtful and sensitive care, hospitality and friendship.

Swinton is passionately devoted to exploring as many facets and dynamics of lament as he can. He wants to show that lamentation provides a practical set of instructions by which Christians can express their emotions when they suffer atrocity and trauma. Lamentation gives a new and clear voice to those who suffer. Lamentation is, above all, an important means of letting out all the pent-up frustration, anger, pain, resentment, rage, brokenness and grief that accompany our suffering. It is, in short, a 'pastoral practice that is crucial for practical theodicy',[128] because it ultimately enables individuals and churches to find healing and wholeness, hope and the ability to worship God despite the feelings of alienation and exile that arise when we suffer (Ps 137:4).

When it comes to forgiveness, Swinton argues that the tortured, bleeding and broken body of Christ on the cross gives a new epistemology of forgiveness and what forgiveness might mean in human relationships. More than this, on his view, the forgiveness seen in the cross presents an entirely new worldview that acknowledges 'evil in all its fullness but refuses to respond to it in ways that encourage further evil'.[129]

As a worldview the cross reframes and refines our natural responses to evil in ways that are counter-cultural but potentially transformative through our lamentation and thirst for justice.[130] The cross is a sign of contradiction to all situations in which forgiveness seems impossible or is refused because it is 'the most radical gift that God calls us to accept and share' in resisting evil. Forgiveness, flowing from the cross, has a dynamic healing power that resurrects 'the humanness of those who have been dehumanised by our desire for vengeance'.[131]

The Church, for Swinton, has no legitimacy apart from this task of humanising the dehumanised, but this rests on the ability of congregations and Christian individuals to engage in critical thinking: 'Unless we learn the practice of critical thinking … we risk drifting into thought patterns and subsequent forms of action that are not

---

128. Swinton, *Raging with Compassion*, p. 129.
129. Swinton, *Raging with Compassion*, p. 164.
130. Swinton, *Raging with Compassion*, p. 177.
131. Swinton, *Raging with Compassion*, p. 178.

only dissonant with the gospel but that can in fact, become profoundly evil.'[132] To take an extreme example; without critical thinking we might regard the leaders of the Third Reich as being simply caught up in an ideology and war machine which was far beyond their ability to control, rather than the embodiment of evil they were. But we might ask Swinton whether we really need critical thinking in coming to this conclusion? Are there no other, perhaps better, intellectual, political and theological grounds for doing so? Does not Swinton's concept of critical thinking simply collapse into a set of questions seeking their own answers? To all this Swinton would reply, I think, that many, perhaps most congregations hardly think at all, let alone critically! What was done in the beginning is now and ever shall be so! The lack of willingness or ability to think and think critically has dire unintended consequences. It cannot, for example, 'raise our consciousness to aspects of ourselves and our implication in implicitly evil practice that we may never other wise have recognised'.[133]

Swinton employs the pan-African philosophical notion of '*ubuntu*.' It comes from the Zulu phrase *Umuntu ngumuntu ngabantu*, which roughly translated into English becomes 'I am because you are'/'I am because I belong' (to the community). Ubuntu took on a particular political meaning in post-apartheid South Africa and in that nation's quest for truth and reconciliation. Here ubuntu was used as an idea in which unity, solidarity and togetherness always outrank any other concept or practical tool in community building. Ubuntu concerns a communal view of personhood:

> Rather than perceiving human beings as discrete, uncon-
> nected individuals *ubuntu* views them to be constituted as
> individuals through their relationships and affiliations to
> other individuals, communities, and ultimately God. Within
> this world-view, personhood is not an individual possession.
> It is a gift that is bestowed on others within community.[134]

For Swinton, human nature is inherently relational. The suffering and evil we experience occurs in the liminal spaces between one person and another, one community and another. Ultimately the inherently relational nature of human being and personhood can be traced to the

---

132. Swinton, *Raging with Compassion*, p. 180.
133. Swinton, *Raging with Compassion*, p. 183.
134. Swinton, *Raging with Compassion*, p. 202.

images of God as relational: a) God as a Unity in Trinity and a Trinity in Unity and b) God in Christ, fully a person, fully God. It follows that human beings are 'made in the image of a relationship-seeking God who is Love'.[135]

Swinton includes these understandings of human being and person-hood in what becomes a theology of friendship within his theodicy. Friendship is, according to Swinton, the ability to sit with strangers, those who are alienated from and marginalised by mainstream society. Swinton singles out as live examples the friendship needed by refugees and asylum-seekers but so often refused or withdrawn.[136] They are, for many people of whatever political persuasion and even in government, literally *strange*(rs). Precisely because they are 'strange' they are unfamiliar and the unfamiliar often produces fear, hence xenophobia.[137] Swinton seems to think that 'xenophobia' is far too abstract and calls it out as 'xeno-racism'.[138] Xeno-racism is a current and pernicious communal evil that can only be resisted through the solidarity of friendship. If one person is separated from ubuntu ('I am because I belong') everyone is.

What is the model and source for the friendship demanded by Swinton as part of a workable pastoral theodicy? Following Jesus urges us to offer hospitality to strangers. Hospitality-in-friendship flows from our understanding of our being 'in Christ' and the nature of our discipleship (1 Thess. 4:1; cf. Eph. 4:17 and 2 Cor. 5:17).[139] We are called to be the embodiment of Jesus' loving in ways by which friendship mediates love and love casts out fear (1 John 4:18). The power of love to do this is, according to Swinton, the most powerful weapon in our armoury in resisting evil.[140]

For Swinton our ability to withstand suffering comes only from a relationship with the God of Love. There is, I think, a rather nasty consequence of saying this which, given all that he has said, Swinton surely cannot intend; namely that that those people and religions who do not have or promote God as Love must stew in their own juices of

---

135. Swinton, *Raging with Compassion*, pp. 204-05.

136. Swinton, *Raging with Compassion*, p. 229.

137. See https://www.unhcr.org (last accessed 20 May 2021).

138. Swinton, *Raging with Compassion*, p. 232.

139. See also Michael Parsons, 'In Christ in Paul', https://www.biblicalstudies .org.uk (last accessed 20 May 2021).

140. Swinton, *Raging with Compassion*, pp. 240-41.

suffering. They suffer because they do not believe. They can and must continue to do so unless or until they come to their proper senses and enter into the sort of interpersonal and communal relationships needed to defeat evil. Such a position surely causes more suffering, more evil not less.

Swinton cannot mean this because his pastoral theodicy is located firmly in Christian Trinitarian theology and a vast Christological depth. His theodicy is intended, I think, only for those Christians who are seeking to reinvigorate their faithful discipleship through a renewed and contemporary understanding and application of the corporal and spiritual acts of mercy.[141]

Swinton maintains that 'Loving God is the lynchpin of the Christian life and key to resisting evil and ending suffering'[142] Loving God and other people in and through suffering (Swinton's reworking of ubuntu) has the ability to break the power of those forces which can so easily turn suffering into evil. This power is directly granted in and through the Holy Spirit. It is in this way that Swinton's pastoral theodicy offers

---

141. The corporal acts of mercy are: a) to feed the hungry, b) to slake the thirst of those who are thirsty, c) to clothe the naked, d) to harbour the harbourless, e) to visit the sick, f) to ransom the captive, g) to bury the dead. The spiritual acts of mercy are: a) to instruct the ignorant, b) to advise the doubtful, c) to admonish sinners, d) to suffer wrongs with patience, e) to forgive willingly and without reserve, f) to comfort all who are afflicted in any way and g) to pray for the living and the dead. All acts of mercy, whether corporal or spiritual are, I think, matters of self-giving. The 'Angelic Doctor' St Thomas Aquinas certainly thought of them in this way and linked them to alms-giving because the word 'alms' is loosely derived from the Greek word for mercy/charity as used by the philosopher Aristotle (see esp. Denys Turner, *Thomas Aquinas: A Portrait* (New Haven, CT: Yale University Press, 2013). For both Thomas and Aristotle the performance of acts of mercy is not simply about 'doing Good' in the building up of a just society, important as that might be. Of far greater importance is that they are precepts demanded by natural and divine law. Acts of mercy in natural law, for example, are always based on the 'golden rule' that we act in ways that we would want people to act towards us. Perhaps the best representation of this is still Mrs Do-as-you-would-be done-by in Charles Kingsley's *The Water Babies*. This now sadly much neglected book was first serialised in MacMillan's Magazine (1862-63). I explored the relationship between the acts of mercy as contemplative ethics in the theology of Julian of Norwich in my *How to See a Vision*.
142. Swinton, *Raging with Compassion*, pp. 76-77.

practical modalities through which the voice of the voiceless can be heard and the narrative of their lived experiences guide us to eradicate all that they have suffered, along with similar experiences of those whose voices remain silenced.

Jürgen Moltmann, *The Crucified God*

The pastoral theodicy contained in Jürgen Moltmann's book *The Crucified God*[143] has its roots in his experiences as a prisoner of war during the 1939-45 conflict. He developed these in the construction of a European liberation theology concerned with the social and economic circumstances of repression.[144] It is now widely accepted that *The Crucified God* is *the* most influential work of theological theodicy in its discussion of the place of the suffering of God in theodicy. This section focusses precisely on that.

Moltmann argues that for any theodicy to succeed it must perceive God as being present and active in the suffering and despair of the world. God is not remote from or apathetic to it. Neither is he a divine sadist or torturer. The problem of evil is not an abstract one. It is not a neat philosophical investigation, but one that raises hard, and occasionally harsh, questions against Christian praxis[145] and solidarity with those who suffer.

---

143. Moltmann, *The Crucified God*.

144. Brian Whitney, *Theodicy: An Annotated Bibliography on the Problem of Evil 1960-1991* (Bowling Green, OH: Bowling Green State University Press, 1998), pp. 317-18.

145. Praxis is far more than mere practice. Praxis involves an ethical self-awareness and a desire to be accountable for those actions we take and do not take. Praxis seeks to encompass theory, doing and being as a whole. The importance of praxis for our concerns here is that it is a set of deliberative, responsible and human moral action(s) which involve the process of considered judgements. In modern Christian political and liberationist theologies, praxis is a moral disposition to do justice, love with mercy and walk humbly with God (Micah 6:8) orientated to a 'just and equal sharing of those things which earth affords' as Fred Kann's hymn 'For the Healing of the Nations' has it. This hymn is widely in the public domain but readers may also wish to consult www.hopepublishing.com (last accessed 21 May 2021). Christian praxis goes further. It does not rest content with a just and equal sharing but makes a preferential option for the poor in order to bring it about.

Christian praxis in the face of evil raises two interrelated questions which by now are very familiar to us:

- What gives hope and faith in God in the face of such great suffering and despair throughout the world?
- How, if at all, is it possible to continue to love and hope in our suffering and in the midst of recurring despair, distress, atrocity and trauma experienced by others?

These questions are directly practical, directly pastoral and the answers to them must be equally practical and pastoral, having almost nothing whatever to do with the theoretical attempts to reconcile God and evil, as we will see.

As his starting point Moltmann explains the concept of 'Supreme Being' (=God) in theism: 'The divine being is intransitory, immortal, unchangeable, impassible. ... God cannot suffer, God cannot die, says theism, in order to bring suffering, moral being under his protection.'[146] He argues that, because God is impassible 'The God of theism is poor. He cannot love nor can he suffer.'[147] He must refuse to accept this on the same grounds as Sölle; God is apathetic to suffering and those who worship such a God are indifferent to the suffering experienced by other people. According to Moltmann: 'Since Plato and Aristotle God's perfection has been designated *apatheia*.[148] God is good and cannot be the cause of evil. God is perfect and thus has no needs. God is sufficient and thus needs neither love nor hate. He knows neither wrath nor grace.'[149]

But, says Moltmann, in and through the death of Jesus on the cross all of this changes because in the crucifixion we see that 'God and suffering are no longer contradictions'.[150] This is of course true if, but only if, the Chalcedonian formula is taken absolutely seriously. If God and suffering are no longer contradictions there must be a connection between them;

---

146. Moltmann, *The Crucified God*, pp. 88 and 216.

147. Moltmann, *The Crucified God*, p. 253.

148. Moltmann uses *apatheia* to denote apathy. But it is worth pointing out that *apatheia* can also mean equanimity. Apathy and equanimity are not straightforward synonyms. Our understanding of what Moltmann has to say may differ according to which meaning we choose while reading him.

149. Moltmann, 'The Crucified God', *Theology Today*, Vol. 31, issue 1 (April 1974), p. 10.

150. Moltmann, *The Crucified God*, p.227.

and that connection is Love. Suffering is an integral part of the will to live and so to suppress suffering, as so much of contemporary society wishes to do in favour of a life of perpetual happiness free from pain, is to deprive ourselves of a passion for life. Quite obviously that is no reason to extend, prolong or multiply sufferings any more than to multiply sin is to multiply grace (Rom. 6:1). But to aspire to a life of painlessness and perpetual happiness necessarily oppresses others.[151]

Suffering-Love liberates. God's power, says Moltmann, does *not* lie in suppression of suffering but in his embracing of it out of love.[152] Hence the cross is a sign of contradiction to anything and everything that is not love. The cross is planted in a divine solidarity with suffering. It does not abolish suffering, but it can and does overcome a lack of love and through Christ's wounds we are healed (Isa. 52:5).

Whereas for W. Somerset Maugham 'The tragedy of love is not death or separation, the tragedy of love is indifference',[153] Moltmann insists that the tragedy of our suffering is met and carried by divine suffering-love on the cross. Indeed, Moltmann argues that the suffering love of Christ was greatest of all in relation to God the Father who rejected and abandoned him (Matt. 27:46; cf. Ps. 22:1). On the cross God in Christ enters and becomes fully, really and substantially present in our experience of rejection and abandonment. It is sacramental[154] because 'God himself suffered in Jesus for us. God himself died in Jesus for us. God is on the cross of Jesus for us',[155] and thus it unambiguously follows in logic and in fact that 'God died on the cross of Christ.'[156]

This is not so-called 'death of God theology', prevalent around the time that Moltmann was writing.[157] Rather it is entirely orthodox and has been since the Council of Nicaea met in May 325. God the Father and God the Son can never be distinguished or separated. They are

---

151. Jürgen Moltmann, *The Way of Jesus Christ: Christology in Messianic Dimensions* (San Francisco: Harper Press, 1989), p. 151.

152. Moltmann, *The Crucified God*, p. 46.

153. W. Somerset Maugham, *The Circle: A Comedy in Three Acts* (New York: George H Doran Co., 1921). www.guthenberg.org (last accessed 24 May 2021).

154. *The Catechism of the Catholic Church* (London: Geoffrey Chapman, 1994), paragraph 1374.

155. Moltmann, *The Crucified God*, p. 192.

156. Moltmann, *The Crucified God*, p. 216.

157. Matthew Rose, 'Death of God: Fifty Years On', *First Things, A Journal of Religion and Public Life* (August 2016). www.firstthings.com (last accessed 24 May 2021).

never opposed or divided, so the kenosis of the Son is also the kenosis of the Father. The suffering of one is the suffering of both:

> The sufferings of Christ are God's sufferings because through them God shows his solidarity with human beings and his whole creation everywhere: God is with us …

> The sufferings of Christ are God's sufferings because through them God intervenes vicariously on our behalf, saving us at the point where we are unable to stand but are forced into nothingness: God is for us.[158]

God's suffering is an 'active suffering, the suffering of love, in which one voluntarily opens himself to the possibility of being affected by another'.[159] It is in this way that God in Christ becomes the eternal compassionate – wounded – healer.

Conclusions

This chapter has considered the development of pastoral theodicy through an emphasis on the theological thought of Sölle, Surin, Pinnock, Farley, Swinton and Moltmann. Here I will endeavour to draw out some common themes in order to categorise and summarise the main characteristics of pastoral theodicy. It is important to do so because it will influence many of the arguments made in later chapters.

It is, of course, to be expected that the writers considered in this chapter will differ widely in their approaches and centres of concern. They each write from particular contexts and have different theological focus points.

Surin, as we have seen, mainly deals with the practical responses to the theodicic problem and gives specific and detailed reasons for his rejection of traditional answers to the problem of evil.[160] For him, theoretical answers do not adequately respond to the cruelties and despair of the world which so often arise in and from socio-political structures. Only a pastoral theodicy is appropriate and applicable to the alleviation of the suffering they cause.

---

158. Moltmann, *The Way of Christ*, p. 178.
159. Moltmann, *The Crucified God*, p. 230.
160. Surin, *Theology*, pp. 38-68.

Pinnock and Farley write from within the context of the experience of suffering. Their concern is for people trapped in a seemingly endless cycle of extreme and destructive violence. Pinnock is mainly concerned with Jewish and Christian responses to the Holocaust and its aftermath.

Farley takes up this theme and applies it to destructive suffering after the Second World War more generally to suggest that divine compassion, understood as a 'suffering with', provides an empowering force that frees people to resist their experiences of evil and suffering.

Swinton works from within the life and practice of the Christian community, the Church. His focus is on the ministry of pastoral care exercised by lay and ordained alike according to their different callings. To eradicate evil is part of the great commission to all faithful disciples to preach the word and heal the sick (Luke 9:2).

Moltmann responds to evil, in part, through his experience of being a prisoner of war. He famously emphasises the idea of God's immanence in our suffering through the crucifixion. In his *Theology of Hope* he systematically demonstrates how only one of us can save us and in *The Crucified God* argues that only the God who is one of us, one with us, in our suffering and despair can understand suffering and give hope in our wounds and pain.

What then do these theologians have in common?

We can begin by listing some common aspects of their thought:

- Thinking always informs doing but doing (praxis) is the only way to alleviate suffering.
- They all oppose metaphysical concepts of God found in theoretical theodicy in favour of the immanence of God dwelling in the midst of suffering.
- They focus on how and why it is possible for people to continue to love and trust God in the experiences of evil and suffering.
- They all attempt to reconstruct traditional theodicies to shift the emphasis away from a supposed justification of God's motives in permitting suffering in favour of suffering as a lived human experience.
- Thus they agree that theodicy must always strive to attend solely to the agony of suffering people.

By taking these agreements together we can see that pastoral theodicy brings about a paradigm shift away from metaphysics and a discussion of the inner life and motives of God towards a more existential and hermeneutical model of tackling the problem.[161]

These modern theodicists focus on a practical response to suffering from the perspective of those who are suffering in order to advocate a theodicy motivated by a *theologia crucis* where the cross is a sign and symbol of God's solidarity with them through a shared experience of suffering. For example, Surin contends that when people suffer they speak of and feel a sense of abandonment by God, a 'Godforsakenness,' and that only the cross can show why they are not, in fact, 'forsaken' at all. Far from it, because 'the principle that the self-revelation of God on the cross of Christ is the self-justification of God is integral to the "practical" approach to the theodicy-problem'.[162]

Pinnock indicates that a pastoral theodicy must centre on a solidarity with people who suffer, especially those whose suffering is caused, as in the Holocaust, by ideology and its resultant socio-political structures that cause and perpetuate suffering. She insists that only solidarity 'motivates protest and resistance on behalf of victims'[163] and Swinton says that the solidarity which Pinnock seeks flows directly from the sufferings of Jesus: 'Jesus identifies with the sufferer, and the sufferer finds solidarity in the co-suffering of Christ'.[164]

Swinton's emphasis on hospitality and friendship result from this theological reflection marked by 'close solidarity' with suffering people. This is true of Moltmann too, for whom the cross is, as we have seen, the ultimate sign of a divine love which suffers with the sufferer.

Pastoral theodicists tend to focus their work on the suffering love of God revealed in the crucifixion of Jesus and experienced by those who endure suffering. The suffering love of God, divine com-passion, is bound up with what they believe may be the fundamental solution to the theodicic problem. For example, Swinton says that the ability to resist evil and embrace prolonged suffering comes from a personal relationship with God grounded in mutual love.[165] He contends that the power of God is both seen and experienced in the midst of suffering which 'transforms evil not with force or might, but with the practice

---

161. Daniel Louw, '*Fides Quaerens Spem*: A Pastoral Approach to Suffering and Evil', *Interpretation*, (October 2003), pp. 384-90.
162. Surin, 'Theodicy?', p. 246, and *Theology*, p. 142.
163. Pinnock, *Beyond Theodicy*, p. 107.
164. Swinton, *Raging with Compassion*, p. 99.
165. Swinton, *Raging with Compassion*, pp. 76-77.

of persistent, vulnerable love'.[166] This is a good example of what is, in the end, Swinton's confessional theology appealing only to those already within the circle of faith.

For Farley, God is neither impotent nor indifferent to suffering. God is present in his divine com-passion that is redemptive but neither coercive or dominating.[167] It is on this basis that Farley argues that human beings experience divine love through divine com-passion, which, in turn, empowers people to actively resist evil and suffering. She, like Moltmann, insists that God can no longer be accused of being indifferent to our suffering. Like Moltmann too she understands that God's power lies in God's embrace of suffering through love, not in the suppression of evil and suffering,[168] God is a suffering God whose suffering signifies God's solidarity with those who suffer. The suffering God invites those who suffer to open themselves in love to hope and healing.

Pastoral theodicy is an endeavour to reconstruct traditional perspectives on the logical and evidential problems of evil, the primary task of which is to explain the existence of evil and suffering. The task of the pastoral theodicist is to shift the balance of the arguments of traditional theodicy away from philosophical speculation and towards a more existential and experiential level. Pastoral theodicy directs our attention towards the perspective of those who suffer greatly and whose lives have been brutalised and distorted as a result. It emphasises God's love revealed in the distorted and brutalised body of Jesus suffocating on the cross. The answer to the theodicic problem is to open ourselves to full cooperation with divine com-passion and act under its direction.

This chapter has shown that the major questions that any pastoral theodicy must tackle are:

- What kinds of images and concepts of God will help us overcome the suffering of the world?
- How can we deal with our suffering and the suffering of others?
- Is there any meaning in our suffering and the experience of evil and, if so, what?
- How can a theology of suffering and evil provide practical tools that resist suffering and evil in effective and efficient ways?

---

166. Swinton, *Raging with Compassion*, pp. 165-66.
167. Farley, *Tragic Vision*, p. 97.
168. Moltmann, *The Crucified God*, p. 227.

- How can a theology of suffering and evil offer healing and hope in ways that equip and enable people to continue to love, trust and serve God as they suffer?

This chapter has also explored some of the criticisms of traditional theoretical theodicy posed by pastoral theodicists. In their development of a radical division between theory and praxis, pastoral theodicists have tended to overlook the theological point that theory and praxis always need each other to be what they are. Indeed, many theoretical theodicists have made much of this in defence of their own position and as the major starting point for their replies to the pastoral approach to theodicy, as we will now see in the next chapter.

Chapter 3

Key Issues in Modern Theodicy

This chapter will be concerned with three specific issues in the debates between pastoral and theoretical theodicists: the theoretical context in which a pastoral theodicy becomes possible, the nature of God in relation to suffering and the brutal, destructive suffering faced by so many in the second decade of the twenty-first century. These three issues have been singled out from many others because they will become the main points of contact with the medieval theology of Julian of Norwich in later chapters, in which I will argue that her theodicy may make positive contributions to resolving the differences between the theorists and the pastoralists.

The first key issue to concern us here is the apparent abandonment of theological theory by those who take a pastoral approach to the problem of evil. I will argue that theological theory is essential not only to underpin but to make sense of what the pastoralists have to say.

The second issue returns to the perennial discussion of whether God is over and against suffering in some detached way or is intimately involved with it through divine com-passion and suffering love. I will attempt to show that both the theorists and the pastoralists need a concept of divine love in order to provide any consolation at all to those who suffer.

The third issue concerns another look at the nature of destructive suffering but this time by way of the ideologies and socio-political structures that cause and prolong it. I will argue that the attempt to create an appropriate theology of evil demands that theologians revisit traditional Christology and eschatology.

The Problem of Abandoning Traditional Theoretical Theodicy

As we saw in the last chapter, modern critics of traditional theodicy – Farley, Pinnock, Surin and Swinton among them – claim that the theory of the problem of evil should be abandoned, or at the very least subverted, if theodicy is to have any impact on people who suffer. Let us remind ourselves that their main reasons for taking this view are that:

- Theoretical theodicy does not engage in specific instances of evil, such as the Holocaust and its aftermath.
- It condones and conspires with evil by ignoring the ideologies and social structures that cause and prolong it.
- It cannot provide practical support for or consolation to people who suffer and nor does it attempt to do so.
- As a consequence of the above, theoretical theodicy is not only irrelevant to people who suffer; it is immoral.
- It has no place in modern theology because it is merely a set of idle speculations, an abstract game played by esoteric scholars who have little concern for or contact with 'real' people living in the 'real' world.

In the face of these potentially devastating criticisms, theoretical theodicists have not been slow in taking to the barricades of defence. David O'Connor, for example, defends theoretical theodicy against Surin's charge that theoretical theodicy is 'irrelevant to the real problem, immoral, tacitly an endorsement of evil, and undermined by the reality of evil'.[1] O'Connor admits that *some* philosophical questions about the problem of evil *may* be irrelevant to people who suffer, but he insists that this is only a preliminary argument that provides neither necessary nor sufficient grounds for Surin's conclusion that *all* theoretical theodicies are immoral and a tacit sanction of evil which belittles or ignores those same people.

According to O'Connor pastoral theodicists, like Surin, have failed to notice that theoretical theodicy operates on a different level and with different concerns to those at which pastoralists work. Theoretical theodicy *is* in essence an intellectual exercise that attempts to understand

---

1. David O'Connor, 'In Defence of Theoretical Theodicy', *Modern Theology*, Vol. 5, issue 1 (1988), p. 61.

the properties of God in the light of evil and suffering and evil in the world. The central concern is not evil and suffering, or indeed the people who experience it, but *divinity*. So it is that an intellectual response to theodicy is quite different from that addressed to the victims of suffering. It stands in contrast to the individual existential dimension of the problem. For O'Connor the stance of Surin and others starts out from a position, which is really an assumption, that, because of this different focus, theoretical theodicy must always and everywhere be 'heartless, indifferent and acquiescent in the face of real suffering', without, ironically, first considering the distinction that they also make between the conceptual and existential dimensions of the problem of evil.[2]

Tilley criticised theoretical theodicy on the grounds of its speculation and rationalism. He claimed that theory attempts to explain too much while at the same time it almost never takes into consideration the social aspects of evil. Hence, according to Tilley, any and every attempt to approach the problem of evil from a theoretical perspective is not only itself a product of evil, but creates it.[3] In response Dan Stiver says that Tilley is inclined to throw the baby out with the bathwater, to the extent that what Tilley completely rejects may, in some cases, be exactly what was needed. Tilley draws very broad conclusions about all theodicies from a very narrow set of premises. Tilley is therefore extravagant and does not seem to recognise that the problem he identifies may not be a problem for theodicy *per se* but only for poor and inadequate individual theodicies.[4]

Similarly, Michael Stoeber has strongly contended that the harsh criticisms lodged against theoretical theodicies are often exaggerated and polemical. They do not and cannot apply to every theme in a theoretical approach to the problem of evil. Theoretical theodicy is not itself evil and it is the claim that it is that should be abandoned, not theoretical theodicy. As if Stoeber were writing an end of term report on a somewhat errant schoolboy, he insists that theoretical theodicy should not be expelled from among theologians and others but certainly 'ought to do better'.[5]

---

2. O'Connor, 'In Defence', p. 64.

3. Tilley, *The Evils of Theodicy*, p. 3 and chapter 9.

4. Dan Stiver, 'The Problem of Theodicy', *Review and Expositor*, Vol. 93, issue 4 (Fall 1996), pp. 511 and 514.

5. Michael Stoeber, *Reclaiming Theodicy: Reflections on Suffering, Compassion and Spiritual Transformation* (New York and Houndsmills: Palgrave Macmillan, 2005), p. 65.

Marilyn McCord Adams also argues that the pastoralists are fundamentally mistaken in their claim that theoretical theodicy is 'both conceptually confused and morally pernicious'.[6] She admits that philosophical theologians of the first rank, such as Plantinga and Swinburne, recognise that their 'philosophical reflections don't automatically work pastoral cures; all concur that the criteria for pastoral effectiveness is irrelevant to their enterprise',[7] but refutes the idea that philosophical reflection is always irrelevant to the problem of suffering – and maintains that it certainly is not inherently immoral.

Barry Whitney chose to reply to Pinnock's criticisms of theoretical theodicy. He claims that her position is itself fatally flawed, relying as it does on the idea that theoretical theodicy is 'epistemologically absurd (Kant), morally scandalous, and harmful, insofar as they condone evils by ignoring their social dimensions'.[8] Pinnock, says Whitney, is especially mistaken in her view that all modern theoretical theodicies flow from Enlightenment thought, especially from the writings of Leibniz and Hegel. This is, says Whitney, simply not the case and it is this fundamental misunderstanding that renders Pinnock's own theodicy irrelevant to specific instances of evil, even the Holocaust to which she claims to respond. Moreover, Pinnock is, according to Whitney, in thrall to the views of Surin and Tilley, both of whom find the writings of Leibniz and Hegel especially objectionable:

> Such theodicies claimed to *fully* justify evil and suffering in a cold-hearted, insensitive and purely theoretical manner that is all-but-irrelevant to individual sufferers in their particular situations. Worse yet, they 'effaced' the social causes of suffering and render protest and other practical coping methods meaningless. Yet, in my view, this contention assumes that Leibnizian-Hegelian theodicy is the model of contemporary theodicies. I hardly think it is.[9]

6. Marilyn McCord Adams, *Horrendous Evils and the Goodness of God* (Ithaca, NY: Cornell University Press, 1999), p. 184. See also Marilyn McCord Adams and Robert Merrihew Adams (eds.), *The Problem of Evil* (Oxford: Oxford University Press, 1990).

7. Adams, *Horrendous Evils*, pp. 184-86.

8. Barry Whitney, 'The Review of *Beyond Theodicy: Jewish and Christian Thinkers Respond to the Holocaust*', *Studies in Religion/Sciences religieuses*, Vol. 31, issue 3-4 (2002), p. 473. See also his article: 'Anti-Theodicy, is Theodicy Itself Evil?' http://drbarrywhitney.com/blw-7theodicy-ld.html (last accessed 7 June 2021).

9. Whitney, 'Anti-Theodicy'; emphasis in the original.

Whitney says that not all theoretical theodicies are arrogant, irrelevant and unjust and so display an intolerable indifference to those who suffer. Of course they are abstract[10] but at least some are both legitimate and necessary because they reflect on suffering in relation to the properties and supposed powers of God. A relevant theoretical theodicy would, on his view, be conducted in an academic and spiritual spirit of humility and would make it clear that any conclusions are entirely provisional; but as things are there are no secure grounds on which to jettison theoretical approaches to the problem of evil and replace them only with practical ones.

So far, then, we can say that at least to some extent pastoral theodicy needs theoretical theodicy to be the thing it is. Indeed, I would argue that the cognitive dimension of theoretical theodicy plays an immensely important role in defending it against pastoral attack. Without this cognitive dimension it is difficult to see how a pastoral response to evil and suffering can have any bite, any real force.

In my view, theoretical theodicy can defend itself against the pastoralists if (but perhaps *only* if) it is able to separate out two aspects of our Christian life – and by extension our Christian response to evil and suffering. We need to distinguish between the way faith guides life from faith as something cognitive. To do so is akin to the distinction between morals and ethics. Faith guiding life gives us strength and a motivation to actively 'do' something about evil and our suffering. At the same time it gives comfort and hope. This aspect of our faith must be placed in the sacramental rituals of the Church and the communal relationships of loving care to be found there. Apart from the sacrament and the community of faith this aspect of our approach to evil remains sterile and at the level of good intention.

Alongside this, but not subordinate to it, we must take the cognitive aspect of faith absolutely seriously because it includes the theories that guide and instruct the faith. It must be based on the belief that God exists and the full content of the three historic creeds that express that belief. A 'shorter form' or 'modern summary' of the creeds will not do. Together they ground and justify any 'truth-claims' we might make about the relation between God and evil and make them explicitly Christian.

By way of analogy, I equate the aspect of faith-as-guide with practice (pastoral theodicy) and the cognitive dimension with theoretical theodicy and by borrowing some of the structures of medieval society this becomes clearer still. Let us suppose that faith-as-guide is represented by the ordinary citizenry of a fortified and walled city. Let us also suppose

---

10. Whitney, 'Review', pp. 473-74.

that the cognitive aspects of faith are represented by those same walls and fortifications. For all ordinary purposes the citizens get on with their hectic lives coming and going and conducting business, family life and worship as they will. They may see the walls and fortifications every day, but it is devoutly to be wished that the circumstances and purposes for which the fortifications were put in place will not come about. And yet the very moment that the citizens hear a rumour that their city may be besieged or come under violent and destructive attack those fortifications become absolutely essential. They may limit and bound the daily activity of the citizenry but they protect and preserve it, so that when the threat has passed the city will be as intact as it was before.

In the same way, I contend, the life-guiding aspect of faith is dependent on the cognitive dimension for its very survival, protection and preservation. The life-guiding aspect may be quite oblivious to the cognitive dimension much of the time. Like the citizens in the walled city the life-guiding aspect may be very aware of the cognitive but, for all ordinary purposes, like the walls, it has very little day-to-day relevance. If the life-guiding aspect comes under attack, however, it then needs the rationality and intellectual justification to surround it which only the fortification of the cognitive can provide. They outline what is and is not sensible, what is and is not acceptable and, properly understood, the cognitive aspect protects and preserves from the ever present (and growing) threat of blasphemy and heresy, seeking to ensure that the orthodox apostolic faith will be as intact as it was before.

Without our cognitive defences the Christian faith would be reduced to the life-guiding aspect alone. As such it would be no more than yet another self-help therapy vying for its market share and an increased target audience. Only the bulwark of the rational justifications arising from the cognitive can prevent this. It is, however, deeply to be regretted that in some places in the UK and in the USA the cognitive walls have been breached by vandals, even in mainstream churches, who would sweep away traditional ecclesial practice – eroding the Blessed Sacrament of the Altar – 'cutting out the dead wood' from our congregations because they have 'no visible fruits' and replacing the ancient Creeds with feel-good, happy thoughts and a rewriting of the Lord's Prayer to reflect environmental concerns. It is deeply depressing to consider what may emerge in the earthly city of God as a result. It will not attempt to reflect the heavenly Jerusalem, because it cannot. In short, our cognitive defences are needed now more than they have been for some considerable time.

Since theoretical theodicies flow from the cognitive dimension of faith, I argue that they fulfil this defensive role by making sense of the problem of evil. Without this defence, a pastoral response to theodicy (a product of the life-guiding aspect of faith) simply could not exist. Thus, even though theoretical theodicies may not *seem* to be relevant to our everyday experience of evil and suffering, they are *necessary* because they orientate our understandings of God and human life. They help us interpret both the universal and specific contexts in which evil arises and they sustain our Christian truth-claim that human life has a transcendence. Finally, they provide the only theological language which has sufficient depth and scope to provide a reasoned defence of the problem of evil.

Let us take another example to see how this might be, drawn from my own experience of major depression a few years ago. My Christian-Freudian therapist no doubt had many theoretical ways of approaching my suffering which at times was life-threatening. Although these theories might have been quite irrelevant to some of the specific instances of my problems they were nonetheless essential in understanding the generality of my depression in so far as and in the degree to which they had the active potential to put an end to its causes. Moreover, the course of my 'talking-cure' and the results would have been entirely different without them. In any event, the theories my therapist employed could not be accused of being sterile, disinterested or purely abstract. Far less did they cause further suffering and evil. On the contrary, together with the creation of coping strategies, they resolved it.

I contend then, *mutatis mutandis*, that theoretical theodicic theory cannot be jettisoned, disregarded or suspended in our pragmatic attempts to understand evil and suffering and to bring consolation in the midst of both. Just as my therapist's theories were unavoidably implicit, so it is with our theodicies if they are to make sense and explain the problems of evil and suffering.

Towards a Defence of Traditional Theoretical Theodicy

The last few paragraphs have begun to set out something of my position in finding reasons as to why the theoretical approach to theodicy is necessary if our understanding of evil and suffering is to make rational sense and provide hope and consolation. I have maintained throughout that theory and practice need each other to be what they are, just as citizens need to be defended from external strife. Here I am influenced by Stiver's article 'The Problem of Theodicy',[11] in which he identifies three groups in the contemporary approach to theodicy as follows.

---

11. Stiver, 'Problem of Theodicy', p. 57.

The first group are those who propose a wholesale revision of theodicy. Marilyn McCord Adams is included in this group because, according to Stiver, she recognises that some traditional approaches (which?) have the effect of ruling out central aspects of Christian thought such as the cross and resurrection of Jesus.

Stiver places himself in this group because it is the only one that is fully consistent and has the advantage of being able to draw on the other two groups. For example, the second, rejectionist group can be very useful in producing a revised theodicy. The importance of this group lies, according to Stiver, in its ability to create a theodicy for Christians and non-Christians alike and provides the best possible resolution to the logical and practical problems of evil. This group rejects a dichotomy between theory and praxis and wishes to find a theological marriage between them. A quotation from Adams will suffice:

> I have meant to chart a *via media* that rejects any dichotomy of philosophical reflection ... and praxis. ... If they are not the same I nevertheless envision a marriage between them. To appreciate their partnership ... it should be enough to consider that personal meaning-making is an engaged praxis ... Yet, engaged praxis is not opposed to theory ...[12]

The second group, represented by Wendy Farley, rejects traditional theodicy almost entirely.

The third group is represented by Tilley and those who consistently refuse to engage with traditional theodicy but do so at the expense of other contradictory elements.

According to Stiver, all theodicists must ask searching questions of the theoretical approach without rejecting it and show how better reflection can improve it.[13] As this process takes place a more balanced theodicy occurs, one which integrates both the theoretical and the practical so that individuals are able to respond to particular evils with as many weapons as possible.

Adams broadly agrees but thinks that the theoretical elements may, like the owl of Minerva, fly only in the evening at a stage following the practical. She rescues this from being a *post-hoc* justification by insisting that people as a matter of fact face and tackle instances of evil and

---

12. Adams, *Horrendous Evils*, pp. 186-87.
13. Stiver, 'Problem of Theodicy', p. 515.

suffering and only afterwards raise questions against it.[14] She argues that theoretical approaches can and do help to bring about lasting consolation and hope, which can equally be regarded as pastoral responses, although this might come about, if at all, only after a long period of time and only once a person has integrated their lived experience of horrendous evil with the goodness of God and their overall *weltanshauung*. Some lived experiences of evil are so horrendous that this cannot occur for they are soul-destroying.

Stoeber agrees with the idea that some evils are so great that they rot the soul and that some theoretical responses have tended to play down, even belittle, the strength of such evils. But to abandon theoretical theodicy altogether would be to abandon the hope and consolation that Adams identified as a possibility emerging from them. It is in this way, he thinks, that love and justice can be reconciled with the evil instances of great suffering. Once this hope of reconciliation is abandoned the religious motivation to make a practical response to evil is lost. Stoeber argues that the wholesale abandonment of theoretical theodicy would entail a number of other negative consequences both for theology and for pastoral care. He agrees with Tilley, Surin and others that some theoretical theodicies have a more or less explicit tendency to demean the lived experiences of victims but, he says, their criticisms are often overstated in the sense that this aspect of theodicy does not mean that: 'all themes of theodicy are doomed to failure or that theodicy itself is evil in principle'.[15] Such an abandonment would also exclude all possibility of hope, healing and redemption of victims. For Stoeber, it is essential that Christians retain the hope that 'God's goodness, love and power, are sufficient to overcome the effects of destructive suffering for the victims'.[16]

Some effective themes of theodicy support the hope for healing and redemption. Stoeber states that in any specific instance of evil or suffering 'one is called to attend compassionately to the victim of destructive suffering, not to speculate about theodicy'.[17] But this does not mean that attending compassionately to the victim is entirely free from theory. Theory supports that attention and offers the hope that victims deserve and require. The theory which underpins the compassionate attention

---

14. Adams, *Horrendous Evils*, pp. 187-88.
15. Stoeber, *Reclaiming Theodicy*, p. 65.
16. Stoeber, *Reclaiming Theodicy*, p. 66.
17. Stoeber, *Reclaiming Theodicy*, p. 67.

gives 'intelligible voice to it'.[18] So it becomes clear that without theoretical theodicy the secure basis from which to offer hope and healing is lost. Theoretical theodicy is necessary, though never sufficient, to support the ongoing task of standing alongside victims in and after their traumas.

To summarise this section: theologians who wish to abandon theoretical theodicy have not provided sufficient evidence to support their claims that theoretical theodicy is inherently immoral, irrelevant to victims of suffering and produces other evils. Their desire to abandon all theoretical theodicy is inappropriate and mistaken. Theoretical theodicy protects and defends pastoral approaches to the problem of evil. Nevertheless theoretical theodicy must strive to improve and find ways to answer these criticisms. One way in which theoretical theodicy might do this is by drawing on the passion, death and resurrection of Jesus more closely and clearly and by linking this to the Christian belief in the resurrection of the dead and the life everlasting.

Does God Suffer?

A key aspect of the debate between pastoral and theoretical theodicists is whether or not God suffers. On the one hand there are those who hold to the 'divine impassibility hypothesis', which says that God cannot experience suffering and pain. Nor is he directly involved in the traumatic effects of horrendous evils and everyday suffering. If he was, he would no longer be God, but become simply another member of all created things which undergo change, decay and corruption.

One the other hand there are those who prefer the 'passibility hypothesis' where God not only feels the suffering and joy of the world but experiences it – supremely, of course, in the crucifixion and resurrection of Jesus. God not only knows all true propositions and properties of the world, he has a subjective experience of suffering and evil because he continues to be at work in and through all creation. This is an essential part of what it means to say that God reconciles the world to himself. That reconciliation cannot come about by any other means than through his direct experience of suffering and evil.

In this section, then, I will discuss the merits, or otherwise, of both positions by contrasting the views of Ronald Goetz and Thomas Weinandy with those of Marcel Sarot and Adrio King. The passible position is currently gaining much traction especially among those who study religious experience as a phenomenon. Goetz identified four

---

18. Stoeber, *Reclaiming Theodicy*, p. 66.

reasons for this: '(1) the decline in Christendom (2) the rise of democratic aspiration (3) the problem of evil and suffering as they relate to the scientific understanding of natural history and to the peculiar impact of suffering on the modern consciousness and (4) the reappraisal of the Bible in the light of all of the above'.[19] Weinandy agrees and believes that, 'with the demise of nineteenth century optimism and in the face of the social suffering caused by the Industrial Revolution and in the agony of World War 1, the passibility of God found a natural cultural climate in which to sprout'.[20]

He argues that in a culture in which compassion and empathy are the dominant virtues it is tempting to think of God as encapsulating both: he suffers because we suffer. This may be due, as Anastasia Foyle has suggested, to a perceived increase in evil and suffering.[21]

Marcel Sarot is in favour of passibilism and suggests that the idea of a suffering God might have been the orthodox Christian position had not the early Church Fathers rejected it on the grounds that they did not want to surrender God's unconditionality.[22] This rejection was unnecessary and contrary to scripture: 'the scriptures refer to God as feeling and as emotionally involved, and early Christianity has generally recognised this'.[23]

Weinandy contends that this critique of the Church Fathers misunderstands their motives and intentions. It also implies that impassibility is always negative. It is not. For Weinandy the Fathers were concerned to defend the otherness of God. To do otherwise would be to collapse the creator into the creature he had created. So the Fathers attributed impassibility to God in order to protect and enhance his all-pervasive loving goodness and compassion.[24] Here Weinandy takes a stance in line with the traditional and Thomistic concept of God as the

---

19. Ronald Goetz, 'The Suffering of God: The Rise of a New Orthodoxy', *The Christian Century* (16 April 1986), p. 386.

20. Thomas Weinandy, *Does God Suffer?* (Notre Dame, IN: University of Notre Dame Press, 2000), p. 2.

21. Anastasia Foyle, 'Human and Divine Suffering', *Ars Disputandi* (2005), p. 5, paragraph 1. http://www.ArsDisputandi.org (last accessed 10 June 2021).

22. Marcel Sarot, 'Divine Suffering: Continuity and Discontinuity with Tradition', *Anglican Theological Review*, Vol. 78, issue 2 (Spring 1996), Pp. 237-38.

23. Sarot, 'Divine Suffering', p. 231.

24. Weinandy, *Does God Suffer?*, p. 38.

'Unmoved Mover'[25] who draws human beings towards a love of God and other people.

By contrast Sarot suggests that God is a 'Moved Mover': 'God is not a passive victim of God's emotions, but God primarily is a Mover, an Actor, taking initiatives and keeping control, even though *he chooses* to have feelings and to be vulnerable.'[26]

The passibilist hypothesis presents a strong case that a God of love *should* be able to console the suffering. Only a God who understands suffering from the inside can do this. Only a God who is one of us in the experience of suffering can deliver us from evil. God is com-passionate because he is a co-sufferer and in this his vulnerability is of supreme importance: 'Vulnerability is a consequence of the need-character of God's love: it is exactly the fact that God desires that the human being he loves both lead a happy life and return his love that makes God vulnerable to anything that goes wrong.'[27] Without vulnerability God has no capacity to be a co-sufferer. Weinandy thinks this is dangerous. It erodes the idea that God is perfect to the point of destruction: 'He [God] is ontologically immutable – that is, ontologically unchanging in His perfect love and goodness.'[28]

God is perfectly com-passionate not because he suffers with those who suffer but because his love is freely given, altruistic and always benevolent as it fully embraces the sufferer in her troubles: 'God's compassion is most clearly manifested in His divine power and goodness through which he overcomes evil and the suffering it causes.'[29] Since Jesus is God and God is impassible it must follow that the divine nature of Jesus is also impassible. This raises another important aspect of the debate between the two camps we are examining. Did Jesus suffer only in his human nature? If so, how is he still God on the cross? At which point in the passion does the divine nature flee, and why? Was it during his prayer in the Garden and so caused his agony, or was it on the cross expressed in his cry of 'My God, my God, why have you forsaken me?' Theologians who object to the passibility hypothesis claim that Jesus' experiences cannot be ascribed to God because the Bible does not say so. The Bible, they say, makes a clear distinction between Jesus and God. Jesus, not

---

25. For an excellent summary of this idea see www.philosophy.lander.edu (last accessed 10 June 2021).
26. Sarot, 'Divine Suffering', p. 237; my emphasis added.
27. Sarot, 'Divine Suffering', p. 236.
28. Weinandy, *Does God Suffer?*, p. 38.
29. Weinandy, *Does God Suffer?*, p. 40.

God, suffered, was crucified, died and was buried. They criticise the passibility hypothesis for having (deliberately?) overlooked this and with it the implications for the systematic understanding of the doctrine of the Trinity.

König raises an obvious question against these criticisms: 'If God cannot change in any way whatsoever, how could God the Son become what he had not been previously – a man?'[30] König contends that where the mutability of God is absolutely denied the doctrine of the incarnation of the divine Logos is also called into question. He shows that theologians who favour the passibilist hypothesis generally agree that the biblical testimony of Jesus' suffering also applies to his divine nature. Thus, if God the Son became a human being, he must also have suffered and died. If we deny this, says König we have the greatest possible difficulty in understanding the doctrine of the two natures in one person, Jesus Christ.[31]

Critics of the passibilist hypothesis suggest that its conclusions may not be a theodicy at all but merely a systematic framing of the personal experience of those who hold this view which they then project onto God in a Feuerbachian or Freudian sense.[32] Consolation and hope arise only because evil and suffering is given away.

Unsurprisingly, passibilists rebut this charge on the grounds that an impassible God is an apathetic God. The co-suffering of God can and does reduce the threatening character of suffering itself and supports those who suffer by changing their view of it. This is made clear in the theologies of Sölle and Moltmann. They both, for different reasons, affirm that God suffers *with* human beings: God suffers with the oppressed. God is always sympathetically and empathetically involved with them.

For Sölle, as we have noted, an apathetic God is incapable of leading human beings to an authentic understanding of suffering because such a God is 'the almighty ruler whose *only relationship* with suffering is that he causes it or sends it or takes it away'.[33]

---

30. Adrio Konig, 'The Idea of a Crucified God: Some Systematic Questions', *Journal of Theology for South Africa*, Vol. 39 (1992), pp. 58-59.

31. Konig, 'Idea', p. 60.

32. For a useful summary of the positions of Feuerbach and Freud on the matter of religious projection see www.didymus.org (last accessed 11 June 2021).

33. Sölle, *Suffering*, p. 143, and for more on the incapabilities of an apathetic God see pp. 41-48; my emphasis added.

If God is not a suffering God we cannot properly understand the properties of God in relation to evil and suffering, especially the suffering of innocent victims of genocide. Impassibilists, such as Henri Simoni, say that it is quite the other way about: 'If God were a suffering God, that would make theodicy even more difficult, for we would have to justify why God is not only a sadist but also a masochist, that is, we would have to explain why the divine essence would create a world that would cause it pain.'[34]

Why yes of course! That is the essence of the whole theodicic problem, so perhaps this does not enhance the debate or make a particularly strong contribution to it. Nevertheless, Goetz says that one of the problems in the debate between the passibilist and impassible hypotheses is that it raises more questions about the nature of atonement and redemption than either can adequately answer.[35] Passibilists argue that it is 'the impassible position that makes atonement and redemption improbable because they imply, if not entail, a change in God to bring these things about. Impassibility is incompatible with a com-passionate God.'[36]

It is to the Compassion of God that we now turn.

God's Compassion

In his book *A Theology of Compassion: Metaphysics of Difference and the Renewal of Tradition* Oliver Davies says that compassion is 'the recognition of another's condition, entailing a degree of participation in the suffering of the other, an embrace of that fellow-suffering, and a preparedness to act on their behalf'.[37] He illustrates this by looking at a number of synonyms for compassion in different ancient and modern languages and concludes that: 'Where these words are used, we can be sure that the notion of fellow-suffering is implied.'[38]

Robert C. Roberts distinguished between different kinds of love bound up in the notion of 'fellow-suffering'. It is not friendship nor affection. It

---

34. Henri Simoni, 'Divine Passibility and the Problem of Radical Particularity: Does God Feel your Pain?', *Religious Studies,* Vol. 33, issue 3 (September 1997), p. 346.

35. Goetz, 'Suffering of God', p. 38.

36. Simoni, 'Divine Passibility', p. 344.

37. Oliver Davies, *A Theology of Compassion: Metaphysics of Difference and the Renewal of Tradition* (Grand Rapids, MI: William B. Eerdmans Publishing Co., 2001), p. 233.

38. Davies, *Theology of Compassion*, p. 234.

is not the mutual loving and self-giving of sex. Nor is it to be confused with the pastoral care given in the Church. The meaning of compassion is derived from the meaning of the actions accompanying it. It is fundamentally based on a fellowship *in* suffering.[39] This may lead us to think that compassion and empathy are closely aligned insofar as they flow from an acceptance that suffering is an inseparable part of human identity.

Stoeber certainly sees a clear link here but says that empathy and compassion have different starting and end points:

> Empathy is the ability to reach out to another person and feel her or his emotions – to relate to another person intimately through a sharing of their thoughts and feelings ... empathy is a feeling-along-with-others.

> Compassion is a feeling-along-with the suffering of others through a framework of love. Genuine compassion involves an affectionate sharing of the suffering of another person, whereby the sufferer might feel the support and receive it in this interchange of love. The exchanged love ... soothes and consoles the sufferer, which stimulates healing.[40]

Empathy and compassion oppose apathy and indifference and the sadism mentioned earlier. Together they constitute 'passionate stances towards others, where distorted pleasure is experienced in ... identification with their suffering experiences',[41] so that genuine empathetic compassion is 'the projection of one's personality upon the consciousness of another person who is suffering, and experiencing, comprehending and actively responding to ... suffering ... within a consciousness of empathetic love'.[42]

In Christianity, compassion is not only an altruistic emotion and a social virtue[43] but is inseparable from the concept of God and his care for all that he has made. God is intolerant of sin but cannot separate

---

39. Robert C. Roberts, 'Compassion', *The Christian Century* (5-12 January 1983), p. 14.
40. Stoeber, *Reclaiming Theodicy*, pp. 27 and 29.
41. Stoeber, *Reclaiming Theodicy*, p. 38.
42. Stoeber, *Reclaiming Theodicy*, pp. 37-38.
43. Brian Carr, 'Pity and Compassion as Social Virtues', *Philosophy*, Vol. 74, issue 289 (July 1999), pp. 411 and 419.

himself from those who do. If he could he would not be God. Indeed, God is with us (Emmanuel) not despite our weakness, our suffering and sin, but *precisely because of it.* God *chooses to identify with us* because only one of us can save us and that salvation is compassionate love. God 'took on human nature, including ... susceptibility to pain and death, the whole range of sadness and joy and even, mysteriously, sin'.[44] This understanding of the incarnation is the foundation of all Christian thought and the New Testament indicates how we might understand the outcomes of that through history. It symbolises the efficacy of divine power in historical existence because the incarnation itself is a symbol of redemptive power in history as a compelling paradigm of divine presence.[45] Divine compassion has its source and its apotheosis in the crucifixion of Jesus. The cross shows that the property of God is always to have mercy[46] and to enter into our suffering. The cross is *the* event in God's loving solidarity with all who suffer in a suffering world.

I have argued elsewhere that for some Christians an awareness of this divine compassion in suffering can, and does, lead to an *imitatio Christi* that identifies personal suffering with the God who suffers and grants healing power. Whereas I suggested that this healing power is available to all Christians Stoeber seems to suggest that it is largely confined to mystics such as, say, Julian of Norwich, Meister Eckhart and St Ignatius of Loyola:

> There is a profound healing power that some spiritually minded Christians[47] become aware of *mystically,* – a consciousness arising from deep in one's heart of the presence of Christ's own pained appreciation of our suffering. ... It is a consciousness of Jesus' deep sorrow for one's own heartache, which inexplicably consoles me in a radically healing way. It is not simply an awareness of Jesus' suffering, but rather a heartfelt appreciation of his compassionate suffering for us and with us. ... This awareness ... moves the sufferer into a profound and mysterious healing grief of self and gives ... the feeling and knowledge that she does suffer alone, that God

---

44. Roberts, 'Compassion', pp. 16-17. Cf 2 Cor. 5:21, Phil. 2:5-11 and 1 Pet. 2:22.

45. Farley, *Tragic Vision*, pp. 113-14.

46. Prayer of Humble Access. The Order for the Administration of the Lord's Supper or Holy Communion. Book of Common Prayer 1928. www.justus. anglican.org/resources/bcp/1928/HC.htm (last accessed 15 June 2021).

47. I am tempted to ask 'Are there any other kind?!'

is willing to die for her and with her – that Christ is present most intimately in her pain, that Christ is taking her gently through her pain.[48]

When allowed to develop, this Christian response to suffering and the consolation that flows from it helps us take a more compassionate stance towards suffering people and the natural world. This notion of divine compassion goes a long way to resolving the theodicic problem insofar as it alleviates, persuades and above all reconstructs it. It has the distinct advantage of moving the problem away from its place in abstract theology into the realm of lived and shared experience; an experience shared by both people and God. That God transforms evil and suffering from the inside through the incarnation may be the only authentic response to evil in the world. Certainly, it may be the most practical or pastoral. This may be true even for Sölle, who after the Holocaust rightly struggled with the orthodox concept of the impassibility and omnipotence of God[49] but who nevertheless believes that God's solidarity with us has a profound healing and reconciling power. It leads to a new understanding of the power of God and a renewal of our concern for each other's welfare.

Jürgen Moltmann's crucified God also poses the question of divine power and compassion. For him, the cross as a critical theory of God tells us of the property of compassionate solidarity which always already ensures that the charges of divine apathy and remoteness no longer stick. God in Jesus undergoes vulnerability, suffering and death 'in order to heal, to liberate and confer new life'.[50] God's power does not lie in his ability to suppress evil, but in his loving embrace of it. It is not 'as a triumphalistic conquering power that strives to annihilate evil, but rather as a suffering presence that transforms evil not with force or might, but with persistent, vulnerable, love'.[51]

Even if the inclusion of divine compassion in the problem of evil goes a long way to resolve it there remains an elephant in the room. We must ask whether to do so is to exchange God's sovereignty in favour of his

---

48. Stoeber, *Reclaiming Theodicy*, p. 50. As we will see below, Stoeber at this point seems to be rewriting Julian's entire theodicy.

49. Dorothee Sölle, 'God's Pain and our Pain', in Marc Ellis and Otto Maduro (eds.), *The Future of Liberation Theology* (Maryknoll, NY: Orbis Books, 1989), p. 332.

50. Jürgen Moltmann, *The Church in the Power of the Spirit: A Contribution to Messianic Ecclesiology,* tr. M. Kohl (London: SCM Press, 1977), p. 64.

51. Swinton, *Raging with Compassion*, pp. 165-66.

immanence. Have we simply dealt with opposites; impassiblity versus passibility, abstraction versus lived experience, loving compassion and solidarity versus omnipotence and omniscience? Have we, in short, just expressed the problem of evil differently and in terms to suit a pastoral approach and not really made any progress at all? Perhaps we can only do so if we now introduce not only compassion but an eschatological hope as a dimension to the debate.

The following section will deal with this so that in later chapters we will be better placed to explore all the themes considered so far in direct relation to the spiritual theodicy of Julian of Norwich.

Destructive Suffering and Some Responses

> There is a distinction here ... between (1) destructive suffering, which diminishes and hinders the person in some way ... and for which there is no transformative impetus or response in the person and (2) transformative suffering – that which contributes positively to spiritual growth – what we might call transformative suffering.[52]

It can be difficult to distinguish (1) from (2) especially when we take into account the whole context of a life and any quest for spiritual development. According to Stoeber some people can respond very positively to (1) but they are *rara aves* indeed and it may take considerable time to realise that they have done so. It is important not 'read back' supposed positivity which simply was not present at the time;[53] doing so shrouds the victims from view.[54]

Stoeber contends that if these rare birds do make a positive response to destructive suffering it can only be in three ways:

1. Insofar as it can generate 'profound emotional states and moral attitudes' including empathy and selflessness.
2. As it adds to an 'appreciation and passion for life experience that would not otherwise obtain' and
3. As it is required to give a deeper sense of freedom and human dignity.

---

52. Stoeber, *Reclaiming Theodicy*, p.61. If we replace 'suffering' here with sin then we have St Paul's question at Romans 6:1 to which we assume Stoeber would give the same answer as the apostle.
53. Stoeber, *Reclaiming Theodicy*, pp. 61-62.
54. Stoeber, *Reclaiming Theodicy*, p. 72.

Together they play 'a role in inducing, intensifying and expanding the human capacity to love for those who must bear witness and respond to its reality in others'.[55]

For the most part destructive suffering serves no purpose. It is true that God *might* be able to bring some good out of it but then we must ask whether destructive suffering is truly *destructive*. Surely in order to be truly destructive it must have no redemptive aspects at all. Simone Weil's sense of affliction and Adams's 'horrendous evil'[56] seem to confirm this. In all cases it never contributes to a positive outcome for the victim even in retrospect. Adams's analysis of the problem of evil arises from her emphasis on the victim's point of view. She insists that everyone is vulnerable to and participates in all sorts of horrors. Horrendous evils are qualitatively different. They give *prima-facie* evidence for believing that the whole life of the victim has become worthless.[57]

For Weil 'affliction' is an extreme form of suffering, 'a pulverisation of the soul by the brutality of circumstances',[58] as we see in her analogy of the hammer and the nail: 'Extreme affliction, which means physical pain, distress of the soul, and social degradation, *all together,* is the nail. The point of the nail is applied to the very centre of the soul, and its head is the whole of necessity throughout all space and time.'[59]

None of these theologians make the traditional Christian connection between suffering and sin. They have biblical warrant for this in John 9. Extreme destructive suffering – 'horrendous evil' – cannot possibly be understood as punishment for it is the tragic flaw in creation (*privatio boni*). The limits of our lives are not our fault and must be separated from sin. Rosemary Radford Ruether makes this clear: 'Within the bounds of finitude and morality, there is certainly much missed plenitude that is outside our control or decision making; that is tragic but is not sin.'[60]

Even horrendous evils are, according to Adams, intertwined with the tragic flaws of the world. They are built into the conditions of embodied existence and are logically entailed in what it is for there to be a world at

---

55. Stoeber, *Reclaiming Theodicy,* pp. 71-72.

56. For a useful discussion of Weil's position see Ellie Payne, 'Simone Weil on Affliction and the Cross', www.clarion-journal.com/files/simone-weil-on-affliction-and-the-cross.pdf (last accessed 16 June 2021). Adams, *Horrendous Evils.*

57. Adams, *Horrendous Evils,* p. 26.

58. Simone Weil, 'The Love of God and Affliction', in *Simone Weil Writings,* ed. Eric O. Springsted. (Maryknoll, NY: Orbis Books, 1998), p. 65.

59. Weil, 'Love of God and Affliction', pp. 53-54; my emphasis added.

60. Rosemary Radford Reuther, *Gaia and God: An Ecofeminist Theology of Earth Healing* (San Francisco: Harper, 1992), p. 141.

all. Where horror is at the root of human tragedy, sin is a disease from which people must be cured if they are to be reconciled to God.[61] Sin is symptomatic of the deeper problem of our participation in horrors. It is the consequence, not the first cause, of a universe saturated in horror.

Farley also says that we live in a world tragically structured so that anyone who suffers cannot immediately be said to be guilty of misdeeds. Some suffering comes from frailty and finitude. She says that destructive suffering dehumanises us to such an extent that it cannot be punishment. It is not pedagogic and it cannot be modified by eschatological justification. This suffering 'penetrates through the whole person and leaves only a dehumanised rag of self behind'.[62] It 'defines the human being as a victim … a deformed creature whose *habitus* is suffering. All experience is absorbed into suffering and the sufferer is impaled upon her pain. … Radical suffering is the incurable wound of despair that annihilates the future … and withholds … any possible meaning.'[63]

That some traditional theodicies have tended to respond to this utter devastation, seeing it as a justified punishment for original or personal sin, shows that its critics are right to call into question its moral propriety.[64] For contemporary pastoral theodicists especially, the most appropriate response to destructive suffering is not an apportionment of blame or moral weakness (sin) but, like Julian of Norwich, through the spiritual power of the cross and eschatology, as we will see.

Adams says that a proper theological response to destructive suffering is *not* that Jesus saves us from our sins but that he first rescues us from living in horror. Jesus defeats horror and all its life-ruining powers.[65] It is in this way that he 'breaks the power of cancelled sin / He sets the prisoner free'.[66] It is this alone that provides consolation to victims and a confidence that the defeat of horror results in an unending intimacy with God. The defeat of horror begins in the incarnation and comes to a climax in the crucifixion where God rescues perpetrators of horror as well as victims. Perpetrators of horrendous evils are themselves victims

---

61. Adams, *Horrendous Evils*, p. 32.

62. Farley, *Tragic Vision*, p. 59.

63. Farley, *Tragic Vision*, p. 58.

64. For an excellent summary of this neglect and its social consequences see Richard Rohr, *The World, the Flesh and the Devil* (London: SPCK, 2021), pp. 1-25.

65. Marilyn McCord Adams, *Christ and Horrors: The Coherence of Christology* (Cambridge: CUP, 2006), p. 40.

66. Charles Wesley. 'O for a Thousand Tongues to Sing …' verse 5 (a hymn widely in the public domain).

of their fundamental misunderstanding of the dynamics of human relationships and what it is to exercise power and control. The rescue effected on the cross is not just once and for all, it continues in the Eucharist every time it is celebrated. That is why the Eucharist cannot merely sit alongside other liturgies but must reign supreme over them. Indeed, the other liturgies have no core meaning unless they flow from and return to what is effected in the sacrament: 'Christ's self-presentation as food bears witness to God-with us providing for us in the midst of our vulnerabilities.'[67] For Adams, the cross and the Eucharist liberate us from horrendous evils and invite us into a relationship of divine love.

Similarly, for Weil, 'affliction' – extreme physical, psychological and social suffering – can neither be justified nor responded to as a punishment for sin. Afflicted people feel themselves accursed and the affliction of Jesus on the cross mirrors it and absorbs it in order to invite us to a participation in the love that exists between God the Father and God the Son. This is by no means obvious. The cross and its liberation from affliction may be obscured in the hidden places of deadness[68] but is nevertheless always and everywhere fully present as hope: 'God can never be perfectly present to us ... on account of our flesh ... But he can be almost perfectly absent from us in our affliction. For us ... this is the only possibility of perfection. That is why the cross is our only hope.'[69]

As long as we can experience the joy of God's presence in Jesus, we can endure the pain of his absence in our affliction: 'Wherever there is affliction there is the cross. ... Affliction without the cross is hell. ... [The cross] is the only one thing that enables us to accept real affliction. ... That one thing suffices. ... Whoever loves Christ and thinks of him on the cross should feel relief when gripped by affliction.'[70]

Loving and thinking about Christ on the cross is the only path to the possibility of perfection which is a key part of the eschatological dimension in our response to destructive suffering; a dimension that stands at the centre of John Hick's famous view of 'soul-making' theodicy,[71] central to which is his belief in life-after-death. The 'afterlife' is not a compensatory reward for earthly suffering but an opportunity for continued spiritual growth. Evil is 'impenetrable to the rationalising mind', but it is this

---

67. Adams, *Christ and Horrors,* p. 300.

68. Rohr, *The World,* pp. 49-70.

69. Weil, 'Love of God and Affliction', p. 49.

70. Weil, 'Love of God and Affliction', p. 67.

71. John Hick, *Evil and the God of Love* (Glasgow: Collins Fount Paperbacks, 1979).

impenetrability that is itself the key ingredient in the soul-making process: 'The soul-making process begins ... at ... birth, making much or little progress as the case may be in this life, and continues in another life ... until it eventually reaches its completion in the infinite good of the common life of humanity *within* the life of God.'[72]

Hick bases his theodicy on two assumptions; (i) that an afterlife exists and (ii) that its conditions are much like our present lives in which we strive for perfection. 'If this life is all, the sufferings and injustices ... would mean that God is not good, or that we are not part of a friendly universe. From any religious point of view ... there must be further life beyond this.'[73]

Two questions arise from this. Is Hick's intermediate afterlife state in which we still strive for spiritual perfection so that we are made ready for life 'within the life of God' Hick's rewriting of the Catholic doctrine of purgatory from his Protestant point of view? Does the intermediate state allow for reincarnation – a position he held in his later writings?. If the answers are 'yes', and I think they are, they do not thereby undermine his equal emphasis on the importance of this life as a spiritual movement to final completion.[74]

Stoeber follows Hick's thinking on this point almost exactly because theodicy cannot be detached from final life with God. A concept of the afterlife is necessary 'both for a future afterlife healing of the effects of destructive suffering and further transformative opportunities towards the spiritual ideal'.[75] For both Hick and Stoeber, then, concepts of the afterlife such as purgatory and/or reincarnation are important means of bringing about healing from the effects of evil and destructive suffering. They are redemptive. Afterlife speculation suggests that, despite our experience of evil, divine love can be defended in the face of it, giving a hope that good will eventually triumph. Divine love is indispensable for the creation of an effective theodicy but a clear emphasis has been missing, they argue, in most theodicies since Augustine of Hippo. Only divine love gives hope of redemption from evil because it is only this that takes the reality of evil and suffering seriously.

---

72. Hick, *Evil and the God of Love,* p. 374; my emphasis added. Hick's use of the word 'within' is curious. Is he indicating a belief in *theosis?*

73. John Hick, *The New Frontier of Religion and Science: Religious Experience, Neuroscience and the Transcendent* (New York and Houndsmills: Palgrave Macmillan, 2010), p. 198.

74. Hick, *New Frontiers,* pp. 198, 200.

75. Stoeber, *Reclaiming Theodicy,* pp. 81-82.

As it stands we may speculate as to whether and to what extent this is to fall prey to exactly those criticisms that pastoral theodicists (among whom presumably Hick and Stoeber count themselves) make about traditional theoretical theodicy. We are promised the jam of healing yesterday (perhaps), and certainly jam tomorrow – but never jam today!

Conclusions

These opening chapters have explored some key issues in contemporary theodicy. I began by showing why the problem of evil is a problem and then discussed the clear differences between those who take a theoretical and pastoral approach to its supposed resolution. I explored whether, and if so why, pastoral approaches to the problem of evil required a substantial underpinning of theory if they are to give a coherent and reasoned defence of the existential-ministerial problems they seek to address. I concluded that without such an underpinning pastoral theodicy lacks substance and gravitas. Not only that, but theory, I claimed, can and does provide some consolation to victims of suffering through its many explanations of evil, abstract though they may be. In doing so I argued, under the influence of Stoeber, that theodicy needs to be reclaimed by a far more determined attempt to integrate theoretical approaches to theodicy with praxis. In so far as it has been attempted at all it has been somewhat half-hearted as protagonists cling to their preferences.

I have also explored the nature or properties of God in relation to human suffering – the very core of the theodicic problem. I clarified that it is Jesus only, the incarnate Son of God, the Christ, that is the embodiment of divine love and that it is divine love that 'delivers us from evil'. Divine love provides the means by which we can understand and experience God's presence with us now, even if the horrendous evils we encounter tend to obscure that. God's co-suffering is the main characteristic of divine love and through the interplay of divine impassibility with his passibility we recognise that there are a still a large number of loose ends which cannot be tied together and the question remains whether a 'reduced' sense of divine power can genuinely support our human compassion for others.

More recently, I have discussed the ideas of Adams and Weil as they provide a particular Christology as a possible means of finding hope in our troubles. I claimed that their views required the inclusion of an eschatological dimension which might have been provided by Hick and Stoeber. Unfortunately it appears that their eschatological verification for evil and suffering based on concepts of the afterlife were just as speculative and abstract as anything which traditional theoretical theodicy has to offer.

In what follows I will clarify and analyse how, why and in what ways all the themes encountered in this book so far were anticipated and sometimes answered by Julian of Norwich in *Revelations of Divine Love*. I will show that her spiritual theology has positive implications for the contemporary theodicies we have considered and how what she has to say should be used as a prime resource in and response to the problem of evil. It is unfortunate, to say the least, that her writing has been so overlooked by theodicists for so long. What follows, then, is an attempt to rectify that omission and I do so by paying special attention to her Christology and eschatology.

Chapter 4

Julian of Norwich and the Problem of Evil

And I conceived a creeping fear. And to this Our Lord answered 'I keep you utterly safely'. This word was said with more love and security and spiritual keeping than I can or may tell. For as it was showed that I should sin, right so was the comfort shewed: security and safe keeping for all my fellow Christians. What can make me more eager to love my fellow Christians than to see in God that he loves all who will be saved as if they were all one soul?

For in every soul that shall be saved is a godly will that never assented to sin, nor ever shall. In the same way there is a fleshly will in the lower part that may desire nothing good there is also a divine spark in the higher part, and this is so good it may never desire to do evil, but only good.[1]

Personally and theologically, Julian struggled with theodicy. To Julian, the personal experience of suffering and a near-death experience and the embrace of a loving God during both were of prime importance. In her *Revelations of Divine Love* (hereafter *Revelations*) she describes

---

1. Julian of Norwich, *Revelations of Divine Love*, tr. Grace Warrack, modernised by Yolande Clark and with an Introduction by A.N. Wilson (London: SPCK, 2017), 37:2, pp. 104-05. I will use the Warrack edition throughout unless otherwise indicated. The first number in the references that follow indicates the chapter number (37) and the second the relevant paragraph (2).

her illness in vivid detail and the confusions and perplexities that accompanied it. Any resolution could only be found within the wider context of Christian doctrine, though with some astonishingly radical interpretations. It is in this way that *Revelations* is a unique account of theodicy in which her intellectual arguments always serve a pastoral purpose. In *Revelations* then we find the integration of intellectual reasoning with praxis I called for earlier.

Where this integration is seen and used by all theodicists, far greater light can be shed on the significant issues in contemporary theodicy and just as importantly much of the heat that exists in the debates. Hence the remainder of this book will argue that *Revelations* should be a primary resource in all approaches to the problem of evil. I will show how major themes in *Revelations* make a positive contribution to healing the schism between pastoral and theoretical theodicists discussed to this point.

I begin with Julian's understanding of the Fall, sin and human nature, which show the uniqueness of her theodicy. It is orthodox but not retributive.

Next I examine her view of the body, gender and evil which strongly contrasts with the prevailing notions of her day and often in ours too. It is not that we have bodies, but that we are bodies which, by divine grace, are changed from glory to glory (2 Cor. 3:18).

I then turn to Julian's concept of the Motherhood of God. Even though this has become such a well-worn theme in Julian studies that it has become almost threadbare, I do so because it is an indispensable response to the properties of God in relation to suffering. It is here too that Julian's contribution to debates in contemporary theodicy can be seen most clearly – especially in her devotion to the crucified Christ.

Sin and Human Nature

The question of sin in *Revelations* arises from Julian's understanding that all things are in God.[2] If all things and all events come from God's goodness and are inseparable from God, how can sin exist? 'What is sin? For I saw truly that God does everything, however trivial it may be. And I saw truly that nothing is done by chance nor by luck, but all things by

---

2. It is vital to maintain the difference between all things being 'in God' and as some wrongly suppose 'God being in all things'. The first is orthodox theology – *panentheism* – whereas the latter is *pantheism* which is heterodox and so heretical.

the foreseeing wisdom of God. … Wherefore I need to acknowledge that whatever happens happens for a reason.'[3]

This is exactly the theological tension that lies at the heart of all theodicy. Since God does not sin and since sin was not shown to Julian in her vision she concludes that sin is no-thing. She does *not* say that there is no sin, but that it does not and cannot participate in substantial being. It has no ontology. This leads her to speculate on the ultimate condition of sin: 'But I saw not sin itself, for I believe it has no actual substance or any measure of being, nor can it be known except through the suffering it brings. And likewise pain: this suffering as I see it, has purpose for a time, for it purifies us, and makes us come to our senses and to ask for mercy.'[4]

This does not mean that Julian fails to take sin seriously. To the contrary. She is most concerned with the enduring and destructive suffering that results from sin which is a scourge: 'Sin is a scourge that any chosen soul may be afflicted with; this scourge … beats man or woman, and makes him hateful in his own sight, so much that it is not long before he thinks he is not fit for anything except to sink into hell …'.[5]

As we sink into hellish despair we become so preoccupied with our suffering that faith cracks and fragments our relationship with God. We find ourselves on an ever downward spiral, taking us down into a pit at the bottom of which we deny God's love. Despair and denial of divine love are the most serious effects of sin and are themselves sinful and Julian wonders why they cannot be prevented: 'I often wondered … why sin was not prevented; for then, I thought all should have been well. … But Jesus who in this vision informed me of all that is needful to me, answered me by this word and said "it was necessary that there should be sin; but all shall be well and all shall be well and all manner of thing shall be well."'[6]

A whole industry has grown up around the last part of this quotation and we have now lost sight of the fact that Julian describes her wondering at whether sin could have been prevented as a 'stirring in my mind [that] should have been ignored, but nevertheless I mourned and sorrowed over this, without reason or justification'.[7]

---

3. Julian, *Revelations*, 11:1, p. 32.

4. Julian, Revelations, 27:4, p. 82.

5. Julian, *Revelations*, 39:1, p. 108.

6. Julian, *Revelations*, 27:1, p. 81.

7. Julian, *Revelations*, 27:1, p. 81.

In other words, she wonders whether her question about the prevention of sin was itself an act of despair. That all shall be well is *not* the panacea that the industry suggests it is. Even so, why is sin 'necessary' and what is the nature of that necessity? Unsatisfactorily, perhaps, it is a mystery which cannot be understood on earth. But is it more unsatisfactory than the eschatological verification propounded by Hick and Stoeber? I think not, indeed it is something Julian, Hick and Stoeber share.

In *Revelations*, 14 Julian enquires how God might view sinners and is astonished to find no anger in God at all. This is radical theological thinking even today because, of course, it creates an apparent contradiction: she sees no wrath in God and yet Holy Church teaches that sinners deserve an ascription of moral weakness, blame and even enduring punishment in hell. The whole of chapter 45 is devoted to her struggle to reconcile the tension. Insofar as she is able to do so at all it is only parabolically through the image of the Lord and the Servant which soon follows. The parable is key to understanding Julian's position as to why God's judgement does *not* entail wrath, why sin *can* be beneficial and why all shall be well despite all evidence to the contrary on all three.

The parable is so well known that we do not need to revisit it here.[8] It is through the suffering of Christ ('the Lord') *with* Adam ('the servant' = all people) that Julian asserts the ontological connections between them. In this identification Julian points to her question about why there is no wrath in God and why no blame attaches to people. In so far as she finds answers they come from two different levels of reality, a divine perspective and human experience. When the latter is viewed through the lens of the former it dies away and with it all the harsh judgements and blame taught by Holy Church. This leads to a greater understanding of why sin is necessary: 'For we need to fall, and we need to realise it. For if we never fell at all, we should not discover how feeble and wretched we are in ourselves, and also we should not fully discover the marvellous Love of our Maker.'[9]

Sin leads to humility and our recognition of the need for divine mercy. In sin we accuse ourselves and these accusations and the feelings of guilt that go with them are necessary for an ever-closer union with God. Sin is not only necessary, it is beneficial; it is part of the 'plot' of faith.[10] The charges of contemporary theodicists, considered earlier, that traditional

---

8. Julian, *Revelations*, 51, pp. 141-53.
9. Julian, *Revelations*, 61:2, pp. 181-82.
10. Denys Turner, 'Sin is Behovely in Julian of Norwich's *Revelations of Divine Love*', *Modern Theology*, Vol. 20, issue 3 (July 2014), p. 418. See

theodicy is always based on a juridical paradigm of punishment, do not apply here. Her purpose in writing *Revelations* was to comfort her 'even-Christiens' weighed down by the guilt and acrimony of sin and the fear of a revengeful God, and to place their hope instead on the mercy of an all-embracing divine love. In her consideration of human nature we see how she answers the question as to how a theoretical theodicy might be the foundation of pastoral theodicy. Each needs the other to be rational and to be themselves.

The end point of her consideration of human nature is that it be made one with the humanity of Jesus. This ongoing process, she tells us, is rather like knitting – and it includes the dropped stitches of sin. The knitting she has in mind is double knitting in both our higher and lower natures:

> I saw that God in our nature is complete; in which whole nature of manhood he makes different expressions of it flow out from him to work his will: he keeps our nature safe, and mercy and grace restore and make perfect. And none of these shall be lost: for our nature that is the higher part was united to God, at the creation; and God was united in our nature in the lower part, when he was incarnate; and thus in Christ our two natures become one.[11]

Julian follows a broadly Aristotelian position[12] in which the 'higher part' is our 'substance' and the 'lower part' our 'sensuality'. Both make up our lives and are the features of our soul: 'For all our life is spent in three stages; the first is that we have our being, in the second we have our development and in the third we have our completion: the first is nature, the second mercy and the third is grace.'[13]

The 'substance' of our soul exists in God before time. It is permanent and eternal and has always been so: 'I saw no difference between God and our substance.'[14] Our 'substance' always unites us with God and

---

also his *Julian of Norwich: Theologian* (New Haven, CT, and London: Yale University Press, 2011).

11. Julian, *Revelations*, 57:2, pp. 169-70.

12. See Mor Segev, 'Aristotle on Nature, Human Nature and Human Understanding', *Rhizomata*, Vol. 5, issue 2. https://doi.org/10.1515/rhiz-2017-0012 (last accessed 24 June 2021).

13. Julian, *Revelations*, 58:3, p. 173.

14. Julian, *Revelations*, 54:4, p. 161.

remains one with him throughout our life. Our sensuality is temporal and temporary. It is breathed into us, as it were, at the moment of our conception. Faith brings it into line with our substance in such a way that our entire being is 'filled with joy and blessedness. For we are made for this end and our essential being is now blessed by God and has been ever since it was formed and shall be evermore.'[15] This comes about in and through the incarnation:

> And thus in the substance of our higher nature we are complete, and in our lower nature we fail: but this failing will restore and make good through the working of mercy and grace abundantly flowing into us out of his own natural goodness. And thus his own natural goodness makes mercy and grace work within us, and the natural goodness that we possess from him enables us to receive this mercy and grace.[16]

God holds human beings in an eternal bond of love which can never be broken – even by sin. But Julian does *not* say that people are automatically doing God's will. Of course they are not and yet, despite all, they are still invited to become 'partners in his good working ... through which he will recognise us and give us endless reward'.[17]

In prayerful partnership we learn his laws, observe his teaching and desire that everything be done according to his loving purposes which were since the age began (2 Tim. 1:9).

We have observed that Julian's theology to this point is a response to her seeing no blame attaching to sin and no anger in God. We must now explore how these insights contrast with traditional theodicy and its basis in retribution and Julian's motives for writing in this way. This demands that we consider again the properties of God, but this time through Julian's eyes.

Julian would agree, I think, that human responses to sin such as grief, shame and fear[18] are entirely appropriate if, but only if, sin is regarded as a matter of deliberate rebellion against God. For Julian it is not. In *Revelations*, 14 she tells us plainly: 'For I saw truly that it is against the

---

15. Julian, *Revelations*, 45:4, p. 127.

16. Julian, *Revelations*, 57:1, p.169.

17. Julian, *Revelations*, 43:1, p. 120.

18. Grief=a response to the pain of others caused by our sin. Shame=a response to our violating or turning away from our essential nature. Fear=a response to God's supposed anger towards us.

nature of his almightiness to be angry, for he is nothing other than goodness; our soul is united with him who is utter goodness, and between God and the soul is neither anger nor even forgiveness in his sight.'[19]

Anger is impossible for God because 'Anger is opposed to peace and love in such a way as to be incompatible with the integrity of God's love, contrary to the nature of his power, wisdom and goodness.'[20] Julian saw no wrath in God and so was perplexed by the theology of her day which did. The parable of the Lord and the Servant was one way to resolve the problem. Here 'the Fall' is an accidental separation from God, not a deliberate act of rebellion. Sin arises from ignorance and weakness but rarely as a wilful act of depravity. God's response to both 'the Fall' and our sin is pity not blame and so he becomes our compassionate healer not angry judge. Jantzen has argued that this also contrasts Julian theology with all theories of atonement by substitutory sacrifice on the part of Christ.[21]

God does not blame us but despite (or even because of) our wretchedness, loves us and keeps us in exactly the same way as he looks on the humanity of Jesus. I agree with Adams that to take any other view runs the risk of reinventing the worst versions of the doctrine of reprobation, producing an image of God that would undermine all notions of confidence, hope and trust.[22] So we must recognise that Julian's image of God as the only necessary being with all the traditional predicates which follow from it leads us to an emotional triumph of trust over mistrust, of hope over despair and love in and through our horrors, though we may not be fully aware of it at the time.

For Julian, human beings are enclosed in the uterus of God's love. Love provides all the food we need to develop and grow. God's love is the umbilical cord that holds us securely in place such that God tells Julian that he keeps us utterly safely.[23] God's love is never distant but is always present to us and appropriate for our needs, moment by moment.

This presents a formidable challenge to our usual concept of God, for if love is the essence of God's very being, all the other predicates,

---

19. Julian, *Revelations*, 46:3, p. 129.
20. Marilyn McCord Adams, 'Julian of Norwich on the Tender Loving Care of Mother Jesus', in Kelly James Clark (ed.), *Our Knowledge of God: Essays in Natural and Philosophical Theology* (Dordrecht: Kluwer Academic Publishers, 1992), p. 205.
21. Jantzen, *Julian of Norwich*, p. 198.
22. Adams, 'Tender Loving Care', p. 210.
23. Julian, *Revelations*, 37:1, p. 104.

omniscience, omnipotence and so on, must be read in the light of it. In the parable of the Lord and the Servant Julian tussles with what this might mean and she concludes that divine love is always *with* the beloved as a friend and companion, such that all notions of dominion, sovereignty or God as an overmighty wrathful avenger must fall away. We can say then that Julian's primary purpose in writing her spiritual theology was a pastoral one. Through it she encourages trust in a God whose very being is love, not anger. This and her views on human nature, substance, sensuality, sin and guilt are directly relevant to the problems in contemporary theodicy we looked at above. The same is true of her understanding of the human body in relation to suffering and evil.

Human Bodies, Suffering and Evil

Julian's understanding of our bodies in relation to suffering and evil is wholly different both from the classical view she inherited and from the medieval theology which surrounded her. She regarded sex and gender, the body and sin, to be interconnected and embedded this interconnectedness in her theodicy – especially as suffering and evil impacts on women[24] – and believed that destructive suffering is a social and ideological construct worsened by some untenable Christian attitudes. All this looks very modern but it is essential not to project our agendas on to her by reading in, reading back. Even so, it is plain, I think, that Julian utterly rejected any and every notion of spiritualistic dualism; that is, the preference of eternity over time and soul over body. These are an exotic import into Christianity from some parts of ancient Greek philosophy and literature. They have a long history in Christianity but they are not themselves Christian.[25] As Jungling and Ruether have separately pointed out, on this view the body is not only a source of evil, it is itself evil. The body is always in conflict with the soul and seeks to destroy it. This is dangerous and commits the Manichaean heresy. What is required is to see that *both* the body and the soul are definitive of what a human being is.[26]

---

24. For more on how suffering and evil may affect women in unique ways see Hernandez, *Early Modern Women and the Problem of Evil*.

25. James Nelson, *Between Two Gardens: Reflections on Sexuality and Religious Experience* (Cleveland, OH: The Pilgrim Press, 1983), p. 6.

26. Laurie A. Jungling, 'Passionate Order, Order and Sexuality in Augustine's Theology', *Word and World Theology for Christian Ministry*, Vol. 27 (Summer 2007), pp. 317-18 and 322. Rosemary Radford Ruether, 'Sex in the

Julian regards our personhood in this way. We are enclosed in the goodness of God: 'For as the body is clad in clothing, and the flesh in the skin, and the bones in the flesh, and the heart in the body's core, so are we soul and body, clad in the goodness of God, and held closely to him.'[27] It is through the soul and the body working in harmony that we experience the joy of all created things, for God made it; he keeps it and loves it. Our souls and bodies, as part of creation, are similarly made, kept and loved and it is the purpose of our humanity to bear witness to that to one another, thus increasing the experience of joy. Julian's positive view of the material world and our humanity within it stems directly from her view of the incarnation. Just as according to the Chalcedonian formula Christ had two natures, divine and human, so do we (body and soul) and in this way we are united with him.[28] It is this which makes us 'sensual': 'As soon as our soul is breathed into our body, thereby making us sensory beings, at once mercy and grace begin to work, taking care of us and keeping us with pity and with love …'.[29]

For Julian, then, the 'city of God' is not some fabled abstract utopia beyond the world but is built in the very core of our being – including our capacities to sin and do evil. That enables Jesus to rule in our lives and his presence in our dual natures grants the gifts and fruits of the Holy Spirit (1 Cor. 12/Gal. 5:22-23) so that our body and soul are increasingly bound together and seek and move towards an ever closer union with God.[30]

As I have argued elsewhere[31] Julian's theology of the body began with images of the incarnation and was developed by Christ's experience of destructive suffering on the cross shown in her visions. If suffering is redeemed by Christ the body must have an inherent value worth dying for. Thus human bodies are reconciled to God through the belief that Christ is the cure for suffering. Faith in God naturally leads us to an acceptance and a delight in our bodies as not only capable of a cure but worthy of it, such that our pain and suffering might be a vehicle for an *imitatio Christi*. Ultimately this is a message of hope when we suffer or

---

Catholic Tradition', in Lisa Usherwood (ed). *The Good News of the Body: Sexual Theology and Feminism* (New York: New York University Press, 2000), pp. 42-43.

27. Julian, *Revelations,* 6:5, p. 15.

28. Julian, *Revelations,* 57:1 and 2, p. 169.

29. Julian, *Revelations,* 55:2, p. 163.

30. Julian *Revelations,* 55:4, p. 164.

31. See my *Julian of Norwich: Apostle of Pain.*

experience evil. It gives bodily solace not just a spiritual one.[32] This is not in contrast to medieval theology, which is commonly but wrongly supposed to have had a hatred of the body, but entirely consistent with it – as both Caroline Walker Bynum and Ellen Ross have separately shown.[33]

I noted that Julian's positive theology of the body is grounded in the dual nature of Christ in the incarnation. When we look closely we see that the incarnation has profound implications for our embodied existence as a psychosomatic union of body and soul. The insistence on the dual nature of Christ overcomes any human feelings of alienation of body from soul or vice versa.[34] Jantzen argued that Julian's understanding of the incarnate Jesus acts as the prototype for 'the remedy of the fragmentation between sensuality and substance ... [and of] our reunification and healing',[35] such that for Julian the body is the site at which we have the possibility of experiencing the triune God.

This positive view of the body makes enormous impact on the theodicic problem. At the very least it has much to say about gender, bodily suffering and spiritual anomie.[36] In terms of traditional Christian understandings related to a dualistic cosmology, women were (and are?) always inferior to men because they had insatiable sexual appetites which had to be controlled by men and their inherent demand for reason and order in all things. According to Rosemary Radford Ruether this misogyny may have its roots in Augustine's concept of the dualistic nature of the soul having a 'higher' (rational, orderly, 'male') part and a 'lower' (chaotic,

---

32. Gina Brandilino, 'The Chefe and Principal Mene: Julian of Norwich's Redefining of the Body in a Revelation of Love', *Mystics Quarterly*, Vol. 22, issue 3 (September 1996), p. 110.

33. Caroline Walker Bynum, *Holy Feast and Holy Fast: The Religious Significance of Food to Medieval Women* (Berkeley, CA: University of California Press, 1987) and her *Fragmentation and Redemption: Essays on Gender and the Human Body in Medieval Religion* (New York: Zone Books, 1991). Ellen Ross, 'She Wept and she Cried Right Loud for Sorrow and for Pain: The Spiritual Journey and Women's Experiences in Late Medieval Mysticism', in Ulrike Wiethaus (ed.), *Maps of Flesh and Light* (Syracuse, NY: Syracuse University Press, 1993).

34. Brandilino, 'The Chefe and Principal Mene', p. 102.

35. Grace Jantzen, *Power, Gender and Mysticism* (Cambridge: CUP, 1995), p. 50.

36. For the argument that sexist dualism is intrinsically bound up with the ancient Greek cultural background to Christianity see Rosemary Radford Ruether, *Sexism and God-Talk: Towards a Feminist Theology* (Boston: Beacon Press, 1993), pp. 78-79.

lustful, 'female') part always associated with the body and its sexuality, and so bodily sin. The image of God resides and enlightens only the 'higher' part. Thus a woman cannot carry the image of God in and for herself. Indeed, she can only do so if, but only if, she is considered alongside her husband. This unhappy association of women with the body, 'the Fall' and sin remains a socially constructed oppressive tool in the Christian tradition. It still causes immense destructive suffering for women both in the Church and out of it.

This may be an import from ancient Greek culture into Christianity but Augustine is not content to leave it there. If he had it could be argued against and its fundamental errors exposed. So ingeniously the Christian Augustine claims that the Bible gives warrant for his position, which is therefore infallible and so removed from any and every debate. Judith Stark[37] says that Augustine's concept of a dualistic soul arises, at least in part, from his interpretation of Eve as Adam's 'helper'. This, she thinks, automatically ascribes an inferior status to all women from which there is no escape. Women must accept their inferiority in all relationships with men but especially those which involve sex and marriage.

It is striking that Julian of Norwich does not agree. Despite, or possibly because of, her awareness of the patriarchy of her day, Julian constructs an anthropology which gives a positive view of the body, including female ones, as a first step towards removing the close association of sin with sex and sex with women. Women are no more responsible for sin than men. Sin is not sexual but a matter of spiritual blindness, a refusal to live according to God's commandments. Sin places us in exile from our true selves and God (Ezk. 2:1-5). Throughout her discussion of 'original sin' Julian mentions Adam, but not Eve.

Spiritual blindness is the key metaphor in Julian's treatment of sin and theodicy: 'the reason is spiritual blindness, for he [a person] is no longer aware of God. For if he was continually aware of God, he would no longer be inclined towards mischief, nor towards any kind of temptation or craving which might lead him into sin.'[38] Spiritual blindness is a sickness with two symptoms:

> God showed me that we have two kinds of spiritual sickness:
> the first is impatience or sloth, because we make such heavy

---

37. Judith C. Stark, 'Augustine on Women: In God's Image, But Less So', in her *Feminist Interpretations of Augustine* (Philadelphia: Pennsylvania University Press, 2007), pp. 54-56 and 225-27.
38. Julian, *Revelations*, 47:2, p. 132.

weather of our hardships and suffering; the second is despair or a doubting fear. ... He showed me sin in general, in which everything is included, but these two particular ones were the only ones he specified.[39]

Julian says that impatience and sloth hold the soul and body together in the inclination to sin. This must be so since impatience, as a function of anger, and sloth are both deadly sins.[40] This union contrasts with those theologies that postulate a disruption of the soul which subsequently infects the body. Rather, her theology is situated in the medieval mystical tradition that used sexual and erotic imagery positively to describe human relationships with God.[41] As the parable of the Lord and the Servant clearly shows, her theology refutes the Christian preference for body-transcending spiritualities.[42] For Julian the body is God's dwelling place and so the site of the most ineffable encounter with him (2 Cor. 12:3).

God is experienced sensually. For Julian, the body is good because it, like all things, was created in God's goodness to manifest God's goodness and in this she overcomes the body-spirit divide.[43] It also helps us appreciate that our human destiny is divine life in God as spiritually embodied beings. Our physical sensual matter becomes a divinely appointed means of reaching spiritual perfection. The supposed holiness of the soul needs the holiness of the body and vice versa; holiness by definition is one, bringing the whole self into the unity of the love of God.[44]

I contend that Julian's theology of embodiment and her positive view of the body provides a crucial foundation not only for her own pastoral concerns but makes an essential, though overlooked, contribution to

---

39. Julian, *Revelations*, 73:2, p. 213.
40. See Angela Tilby, *The Seven Deadly Sins: Their Origin in the Spiritual Teaching of Evagrius the Hermit* (London: SPCK, 2009), pp. 115-41.
41. Wladyslaw Witalisz, 'I cuppe and I cuss and I wood wore: Erotic Imagery in English Mystical Writings', *Text Matters: A Journal of Literature Theory and Culture*, Vol. 4. www.sciendo.com/article/10.2478/textmat-2013-0026 (last accessed 7 July 2021).
42. See Kerrie Hide, 'The Parable of the Lord and the Servant: A Soteriology for Our Times', *Pacifica: Australasian Theological Studies*, Vol. 10 (1997), pp. 64-65. This journal ceased publication in 2017.
43. Kerrie Hide, *Gifted Origins to Graced Fulfillment: The Soteriology of Julian of Norwich* (Collegeville, MN: The Liturgical Press, 2001), p. 203.
44. Jantzen, *Power, Gender and Mysticism*, p. 149.

debates between theoretical and pastoral theodicists in contemporary theodicy. This is seen again in her notion of the Motherhood of God in Christ to which we now turn.

The Motherhood of God in Christ

This section deals with Julian's theology of the Motherhood of God in Christ as an essential response to a key question in contemporary theodicy about the nature of God in relation to human suffering. Julian famously used maternal imagery as she reveals the feminine nature of God as mother – an idea that is somewhat controversial even today.[45] Brant Pelphrey maintained that 'If God is "Mother" for Julian, it is impossible for her to think of God as a distant or forbidding judge who seeks to condemn or destroy the creation God has made.'[46]

Bernard McGinn concurs:

> Julian did not invent this language, which had a long tradition, but she brought it to a height of theological sophistication beyond anything found in earlier literature. Christ is our Mother not only because the image of a mother's love helps us overcome the fear of God, but more fundamentally because it explains the nature of our bond with Christ and the source of his constant solicitude for us.[47]

Here McGinn identifies that Julian considered that the main obstacle to progress in the spiritual life is an overwhelming sense of dread towards God. Dread of God is different from the proper awe and fear that is due to God. Dread potentially rots the soul because it leads to despair and despair leads to utter despondency and inertia. Julian's idea of divine motherhood opposes that dread and at the same time emphasises the loving character of the Trinity.

---

45. It should be noted that Julian does not merely substitute God's maternity for his paternity. Julian knew that God is not gendered and that accordingly neither male nor female language apply. Maternity and paternity are valuable analogies such that God is *like* a mother (or father) but no more. The 'is' here is the 'is' of predication, not identity.

46. Brant Pelphrey, *Christ our Mother: Julian of Norwich* (Wilmington, DE: Michael Glazier, 1989), p. 39.

47. Bernard McGinn, 'The English Mystics', in Jill Rant (ed.), *Christian Spirituality* (New York: Crossroad, 1987), p. 204.

Julian sees three ways in which God as Trinity can be understood as 'mother':

> I understand that there are three ways of looking at the motherhood of God; the first is rooted in the fact of our nature's *making*; the second is his *taking* of our nature, – and this is the start of the motherhood of grace; the third is that motherhood of *working* – and in this activity the same grace is spread forth all over everything, everlasting in its length, and breadth, height and depth. All this springs from one Love.[48]

Making, God. Taking, Jesus. Working, the Holy Spirit. In Jesus Christ the whole Trinity is revealed and known: 'for where Jesus appears, the blessed Trinity is understood to be, as I see it'. Jesus, fully enclosed in the Trinity, is our true mother. For 'This lovely word "Mother" is so sweet and so much more in nature of itself that it cannot be used of anyone but *him* ...'.[49]

As Christ he incorporates all people into himself and thus we are *in utero* of our Mother-Christ. Our union and enclosure within Mother-Christ *is* union and enclosure in the Trinity. This image of our being *in utero* leads, I think, into profound insights for human beings as both greatly cherished recipients of divine love and as being capable of being drawn into relationship with the Trinity and there find our own wholeness.

Julian's analogy of Mother-Christ is strengthened by a biological dimension; nurturing, sustaining and compassionate breastfeeding. Just as a post-partum mother breastfeeds her baby so the post-resurrected Jesus feeds us with his real self, present in the Eucharist:

> The human mother may suckle her child with her milk but our precious mother, Jesus, feeds us with himself, ... with the Blessed Sacrament that is the precious food of my life; and with all the sweet sacraments he strengthens us with mercy and grace in great measure ...

> The mother may put the child tenderly to her breast, but our tender Mother, Jesus, simply leads us into his Blessed breast, through his sweet open side, and there shows us a glimpse of

---

48. Julian, *Revelations*, 59:5, p. 176.
49. Julian, *Revelations*, 60:5, p. 179.

the Godhead and the joys of heaven, with spiritual certainty
and eternal blessings.[50]

Divine motherhood makes the Church holy. Since the Church is
Christ's visible body on earth his motherhood births us into new life and
a living hope (1 Pet. 1:3) in the community of Christians as they strive to
establish the conditions under which God's kingdom will come on earth
as it is in heaven. The Church is the breast of our divine Mother-Christ,
the house in which, the kitchen in which, we are fed with her teaching
and sacraments.

The imagery of divine motherhood occurs so frequently in *Revelations*
that we are constantly reminded that we are 'clasped', 'enclosed',
'enfolded' and 'wrapped' in love. These are sensual, tactile ways in which
people are united to Mother-Christ as a piece of clothing is made to
measure: 'our Lord gave me a spiritual sight of his homely loving. I saw
that he is to us everything that is good and comfortable for us; he is our
clothing that in love wraps us, claps us, and encloses us in love, such
that he will never leave us; being to us everything that is good, as far as
I see it.'[51]

Nothing, no sin, pain, suffering or horrendous evil can separate us
from the love of Mother-Christ and is part of Christ's soteriological
function. According to Hide what makes Julian's soteriology unique
is the 'dialectical unity created by Christ's role as deep wisdom of the
Trinity and mother and the reciprocal enclosure between us and each
person of the Trinity'.[52]

As I have argued elsewhere, it is precisely this dialectic that opposes
the Anselmian doctrine of atonement by satisfaction.[53] Anselm is
almost obsessed with sin. Sin offends God because God is a God of
justice. Sin is unjust and so justice demands a penalty be paid so that
justice can be satisfied. By reason of their 'original sin' and propensity
to keep on sinning human beings are unable to pay the price so God
sends in a substitute to pay it on our behalf: the human nature of Jesus
is like us in every way – except sin (Heb. 2:14-15). The problem with this
view, as I see it, is that justice is a rapacious power and power a form of
dictatorial domination wholly at odds with either free will or a loving
worshipful relationship with God.

---

50. Julian, *Revelations,* 60:2 and 60:3, p. 179.
51. Julian, *Revelations,* 5:1, p. 12.
52. Hide, *Gifted Origins to Graced Fulfillment,* pp. 132-33.
53. See my *Julian of Norwich and the Doctrine of Salvation.*

For Anselm the demands of justice and divine love are wholly incompatible, whereas for Julian such incompatibility is quite impossible. Love and justice form a unity such that God's abiding love for people is so strong that he sees human beings as loveable, not hateful. Sin does not demand satisfaction because it has no objective ontological existence; it is no-thing. The differences between Anselm and his (often Protestant) followers ever since on the one hand and Julian on the other are most clearly seen in their different understandings of what the incarnation was *for*. For Anselm, God became a person in Jesus to begin to pay the price of sin: 'There was no other good enough / to pay the price of sin / He *only* could unlock the gate / of heaven and let us in … / … But we believe it was *for us* / he hung and suffered there';[54] whereas for Julian, like St Athanasius,[55] God became a person so that all persons can become *like* God.[56] Salvation, for Julian, is thus the restoration of people to our true nature; to love others, to love God and to be loved in return and in this way move together from glory to glory (2 Cor. 3:18). This is far more than paying a judicially imposed fine for it signifies the complete embodiment of divine loving motherhood, God's yearning for his people which far surpasses all that we can ask or think according to the power working in us (Eph. 3:20), repairing all the damage flowing from sin, pain, evil and suffering.

So to speak of Mother-Christ is to believe that the divine Word (*Logos*) became human (John 1:14) to incorporate all people in him/herself (John 12:32). It is to believe that there is an absolute, eternal and universal union between God and people and it is due to this union that God can never be angry towards sinners and their sin, nor ever will. Julian's insights here led to her insistence that divine loving motherhood is a predicate of God's nature.

In this way Julian highlights rich possibilities in relation to the question of the nature of God as it arises in modern theodicy.

---

54. From the well-known hymn by Cecil Frances Alexander (1818-95), 'There is a Green Hill Far Away'; my emphasis added.

55. Athanasius of Alexandria, *On the Incarnation of the Word*. www.ccel.org/ccel/athanasius/incarnation.toc.html (last accessed 7 July 2021).

56. This is the traditional and accepted doctrine of the Church. See *Catechism of the Catholic Church*, paragraph 460.

Compassion

Julian's entire theology is a commentary on Christ's passion, which is the supreme manifestation of divine love from which all compassion in suffering and evil flows.[57] Compassion is the foundation of our relationship with others and with God:

> And then I saw that each instance of natural compassion that man feels for his fellow Christians ... is Christ acting in him. That same abnegation that was shown in his Passion was shown again here in this compassion. In this were two manners of understanding what our Lord meant. One is the blessing we are brought to, because of which he desires us to rejoice. The other is for comfort in our pain: for he desires us to realise that this pain will be turned into glory and benefit by virtue of his Passion, and that we also realise that we suffer not alone but with him ... and that we understand his suffering ... to surpass so far any thing we may suffer ...[58]

Christ suffers with us, not for us. His compassionate presence enables us to show compassion to everything that suffers. To do so we must open ourselves to God's suffering love: 'I saw how Christ has compassion on us because of ... sin. And right as I was before in the Showing of the Passion of Christ filling me with pain and compassion, in the same way in this sight I was filled, in part, with compassion for all my fellow Christian ...'[59]

McNamer argues that Julian's concept of the inseparable link between sin and compassion is unique in medieval theology and distinctly feminine: 'Julian ... describes her visions of the Suffering of Christ – visions in part generated by the practice of affective meditation and feminised "beholding" – developed her pity for her fellow Christians',[60] because of her focus not only on Christ's passion but also on the emotions of Our Lady during it producing 'maternal nurturance as the foundation

---

57. It should be noted throughout that Christian compassion, properly understood, is not an emotion or feeling but a phenomenological force.

58. Julian, *Revelations*, 29:3, p. 85.

59. Julian, *Revelations*, 28:1, p. 84.

60. Sarah McNamer, *Affective Meditation and the Invention of Medieval Compassion* (Philadelphia: University of Pennsylvania Press, 2010), p. 150.

for an ameliorative, protective form of compassion'.[61] The compassion of the dying Christ and the compassion of Our Lady for her son is the foundation of our compassion for those who suffer evil.

My own view is that compassion in Julian's writing begins much earlier than McNamer would seem to allow. It begins in the three prayers described in chapter 2 of Revelations. The first was to understand the passion of Christ. The second to suffer physical illness and the third to have 'three wounds': true contrition, loving compassion and a longing to do God's will.[62] The link between the three prayers is her attempt to see sin, suffering and evil from a divine perspective in order to create a greater solidarity with all who experience these things. Spiritually naive as she may have been, the young Julian did not pray these three prayers separately for their own sake. Far less did she expect mystical experiences to follow.

The first wound, true contrition, was an intentional refocussing away from self-regarding motives towards God so that genuine compassion for suffering people might become possible. The second wound, loving compassion, is a parallel to her earlier prayer to seek an identification with the suffering Christ. The third wound is the summation and logical consequence of the other two. Thus, Julian's desire for union with God is *not* an attempt to flee from social responsibility. To the contrary, Julian was deeply concerned for all who suffer, seeking to develop an experiential empathy with their suffering as Mother-Christ does.

In the earlier analysis of the debates between those who hold that God's nature is impassible and those who believe it to be passible we saw that pastoral concern for those who suffer is a dominant feature of the latter and a somewhat recessive one in the former. This is not to say that impassibilists do not care for suffering people, only that it is not necessarily among their theological priorities. The remainder of this section will explore what I believe to be Julian's possible response to the impassibilist position. It is important to do so because as Anastasia Foyle has pointed out: 'modern Christians tend towards passibilist theology as a response to suffering partly because reflections upon Christ's Passion and the sufferings of the saints *decreasingly fulfil the need for an empathetic yet transcendent consoler*'.[63]

---

61. McNamer, *Affective Meditation*, p. 162.
62. Julian, *Revelations*, 2:1, p. 4.
63. Foyle, 'Human and Divine Suffering'. paragraph 31; my emphasis added.

According to Foyle, pre-Reformation Christians viewed the saints, martyrs and other holy women and men as their 'soul-friends' and fellow companions in suffering and misfortune: 'People wished to appeal to a transcendent companion who had experiential knowledge of their own ordeal or misfortune with a *profound feeling of kindred spirit* that arose as a result of the shared experience.'[64] The suffering of spiritual ancestors brought consolation to current suffering by a process of prayerful reflection on the commonalities, if any, between current and previous ordeals. The Protestant insurgency regarded this prayerful practice as idolatry and swept it away with strokes of their swords, as we still see in the beheaded images of many holy women and men in our great churches and cathedrals. This was and remains shameful as it derives us of another route to finding consolation, comfort and possible healing of our sufferings and experience of healing. It is shameful too that so few, especially in the contemporary Church, seem willing or able to overturn the loss of this possible way of dealing with the theodicic problem on a personal basis.

As Foyle argues,[65] one of the benefits of this practice was that it ameliorated a callous regard for suffering or a complete disregard of it as we see all around us today. This is, I contend, particularly true of Julian's theodicy. It radically opposes any and every attempt to disregard the seriousness of sin, suffering and evil and condemns our callousness towards it. Moreover, for our present purposes it helps us contextualise (and so put into perspective) recent trends in theodicy – including the impassibility debate. That is, Christ's experience of suffering and ours are mutually shared in an everlasting love that enfolds us. Julian here is, I think, speaking directly to a concern we considered earlier – the victims of destructive suffering – to which we will shortly return. God suffers in Christ.

Philip Sheldrake disputes that Julian says that God suffers in Christ. For him, Julian only hints that this may be so. Sheldrake's position is curious. While he emphasises that God is indissolubly joined to the human condition through the incarnation he only cautiously mentions that the element of passibility *may* be included in Julian's theodicy and

---

64. Foyle, 'Human and Divine Suffering', paragraph 31; my emphasis added. It is precisely an attempt to recover this lost (and often despised) affinity with holy women and men which motivates many of us who have the honour to be Companions of Julian of Norwich.
65. Foyle, 'Human and Divine Suffering', paragraph 33.

that only in a very vague way: 'somehow, in Christ, God is touched by suffering out of love'.[66] It would be useful to know 'which how' and what impact this might have not only for theodicy but for the doctrines of incarnation and atonement too.

Hide, unlike Sheldrake, has no doubts that God is always moved by human suffering and that Julian says so: 'Christ reveals that the very nature of God is to suffer for love, to take the suffering of humanity into God's own being, to be a saving God through *oneing* in suffering.'[67]

I have no doubt that Hide is right about this and that Julian's parable of the Lord and the Servant makes this crystal clear. In the parable Julian turns her attention to the Lord who illustrates and embodies how God relates to suffering people. God experiences compassion while waiting for the too-eager servant to complete his task. He waits in an unadorned place, a barren and waste ground, he is alone in a wilderness.[68] This is not a portrait of an impassible God or the unmoved mover of classical theism. This is a portrait of a God of pathos who is steadfast in love, sincere and empathetic. God is a responsive God who deliberately unites himself with suffering in order to transform it from the inside, – without justifying its inherent evils. This active compassion, especially the lack of justification for evil, can provide immense consolation and comfort and it is entirely biblical.[69]

In brief, Julian's images of self-giving love in the bleeding Jesus and in the parable of the Lord and the Servant, to name but two, hold a respect for the *mysterium tremens* of God's otherness together with God's response to the pain of what it is to be human. The images show a compassionate God who offers hope in our desolation and the despair which is built into our experience of suffering and evil. Julian believes that only such a God can help us endure all sorts of hardship and offer compassion to others while doing so.

---

66. Philip Sheldrake: *Spirituality and Theology – Christian Living and the Doctrine of God.* Maryknoll. New York. Orbis Books. 1998 p50.

67. Hide, *Gifted Origins to Graced Fulfillment,* p. 205; emphasis in the original.

68. See Julian *Revelations,* 51, pp. 141-53.

69. I rarely mine the Bible in aid of my position, for as my former colleague Adrian Thatcher has shown in his book *The Savage Text: The Use and Abuse of the Bible* (Oxford: Wiley-Blackwell, 2008), the Bible can be a 'savage text' even (especially?) in Christian discourse. Yet the God of the patriarchs, of Moses, of Job and the prophets is a God who has an extremely rich emotional life. God is moved to anger. God loves. God feels compassion, pity, mercy and a concern for the suffering of people through self-giving on the cross.

Conclusions

It is now essential to draw out some of the implications of the themes of Julian's theology considered here for modern theodicy.

Julian's notion of 'the Fall', sin and human nature show that her approach to the theodicic problem provides a theoretical context which undergirds her pastoral concerns. Her theology challenges retributive theodicy. Whereas retributive theodicy is always aetiological, concerned with the causes and consequences of sin, Julian takes a teleological approach concerned with the purpose and end of suffering. Retributive theodicy is always based on an ascription of moral weakness and blame, whereas Julian insists that this is incompatible with divine love which looks on us with pity not with blame and from which anger is entirely absent.

In this way Julian avoids the criticisms that some modern pastoral theodicists have levelled against retributive theodicy and which were considered in earlier chapters. It is her insistence on a progressive unity between people and human beings declared in the incarnation that leads her to the conviction that people are always the object of divine love despite 'the Fall', sin and horrendous evils. God is a God of compassion not by description but by identity, which, in turn, enables Julian to provide innovative ways at looking at the theodicic problem in the light of divine love.

Our physical bodies, the means by which God unites himself with us, join the material and the spiritual. This not only denies the tendency in Christianity to take a negative view of bodies and what bodies do, and with it a wholly negative view of the world. It also insists that people are embodied/spiritual beings in a psychosomatic unity. It is the basis on which Julian strongly affirms the human body with all its sensuality. Julian never takes a negative view of either the body or the world. She is not misogynistic either, despite some of the cultural constructs of her society. Women are no more responsible for sin, suffering and evil than are men. It is here that Julian again avoids many of the criticisms raised by some modern pastoral theodicists which claim that theoretical theodicy is grounded in erroneous sexual myths and stereotyping.

Finally, in Julian's image of 'Mother-Christ' and her/his compassion we see a summary of Julian's entire theology. This too makes a significant contribution to modern theodicy concerning the nature of God in responding to suffering and evil. Julian's purpose in constructing this image is to express the inseparable ontological and mystical unity between Christ and people. 'Mother-Christ' is the one to whom we must constantly turn when we are in trouble or crisis (Luke 15:11-32) and find there hope from desolation and encouragement in despair. We can only do this if we first recognise that we are greatly loved and that the compassion of 'Mother-Christ' is another predicate of God.

So it is that *Revelations of Divine Love* should be regarded as a useful theological resource for all who would construct a theodicy on the conviction that God *is* Love (1 John 4:7-21). That so many contemporary theodicists have neglected to do so has produced what is, in my view, the current somewhat dire state of affairs in understanding the problem of evil in so much modern theology.

Chapter 5

God, Suffering and Eschatology in Julian of Norwich

Having established that *Revelations of Divine Love* is an important but neglected tool in the construction of a sensitive theodicy, this chapter will explore how that is so in relation to two key questions in theodicy: namely the questions of the nature of God in relation to suffering and the theoretical foundation for pastoral concerns.

I begin with Julian's theology of suffering while highlighting its eschatological dimensions, which, I will argue, provide hope for healing. I will argue that the (theoretical) eschatological dimension provided Julian with the motivation to deal with the problem of evil practically and pastorally. Finally, I will show how Julian creatively integrates theoretical theodicy with pastoral theodicy and so overcomes the sad division between the two camps existing in contemporary theodicy which concerned Chapters 1-3.

Julian and Affliction

This section explores how Julian's theology has a positive impact on understanding destructive suffering by being rooted in the passion of Christ and his compassionate love for people. As the previous discussion showed, destructive suffering is just that, destructive. It is neither redemptive nor transformative. It is entirely negative by nature and in its consequences for the victims who experience it.

Some theologians considered earlier – Adams, Farley, Weil, for example – basically agree that destructive suffering stems from inherent flaws that are logically entailed in what it is for there to be a world at all. Our suffering is not always the consequence of sin nor is it a supposed divine punishment for an equally supposed 'Fall' and an 'original sin'. They refute this traditional Christian worldview, which may itself be a cause of destructive (spiritual) suffering. They argue that retributive punishment and doctrines of atonement such as Anselm's neglect victims of suffering and so fail to respond to them. I believe that Julian of Norwich agrees and provides an alternative theological way to stand in solidarity with victims of suffering by insisting on the all-embracing love of God flowing from the God who is nothing but love.

Julian would also agree with Adams, Stoeber and Weil's emphasis on the spiritual power of the cross of Jesus. The identification of one's suffering with that of Jesus (*imitatio Christi*) can provide healing for afflicted people through the experience of divine consolation and presence. The cross is an invitation to live in a mutually loving relationship with God-in-Christ as he reconciles the world to himself (2 Cor. 5:19). This, in turn, leads to an actively compassionate stance towards other people. This is the core message of *Revelations of Divine Love*.

For Julian, the cross of Jesus is 'the supreme manifestation of the love of God'[1] and the central image of *Revelations* and so essential to our understanding of them. The cross offers a theological principle for understanding more deeply what love is and how it is demonstrated. The first, second, fourth, fifth, eighth and ninth *Revelations* directly concern the suffering and the cross of Jesus. They variously trace the course of the passion from the crowning with thorns to the moment of Jesus' death. For Julian, the passion shows that Jesus was treated as if he were no more than a rag. His cross is the collective sum of all affliction in which nothing about suffering is concealed. In a beautiful passage F.C. Bauerschmidt describes this as having 'no interior, because it is at every point of its existence "exteriorized" by participation in the infinite divine compassion revealed in Christ, a compassion enacted in visible practices of forgiveness and vulnerability'.[2]

Julia Lamm[3] has connected this with kenosis:[4] 'Julian's originating revelation is ... a *kenosis* – a self-emptying love, an emptying of all

---

1. Jantzen, *Julian of Norwich*, p. 91.
2. Frederick C. Bauerschmidt, 'Julian of Norwich – Incorporated', *Modern Theology*, 13;1 (January 1997), p. 96.
3. Julia A. Lamm, 'Revelation as Exposure in Julian of Norwich's Showings' *Spiritus*, Vol. 5, issue 1 (Spring 2005), p. 60.
4. See www.newadvent.org (last accessed 12 July 2021).

that is human in Christ so that nothing remains hidden. This image of revelation as exposure in the sense of "exteriorization" – and, more specifically as a Kenotic exteriorising – became for Julian the basic paradigm for divine revelation.' Kenosis for Lamm, as for St Paul (Phil. 2:7), is what incarnation is all about,[5] as Julian expresses in chapter 51. Jesus' experience of affliction in this exposure reveals that, despite our failure and weakness, God's love is stronger than death (Song of Solomon 8:6). If Jesus could have suffered more, for love, that is exactly what he would have done.[6] Salvation comes only through pain. This idea greatly troubled Julian because it is at once both lovely and appalling; lovely because it shows love, appalling because of the depth and extent of pain. Yet pain changes everything:

> And right at the same time that I thought, … his life was about to expire … suddenly … he changed the expression on his blessed countenance. The changing … changed mine and I was as glad and as cheerful as possible. Then, happily, our Lord's words came to mind: 'Where is now any point of your pain, or your grief?' And I was deeply happy.[7]

Julian's vision of the dying Jesus is not one of sorrow, but finally one of joy because at the point of death Jesus seems to smile. Through this Julian comprehends the meaning of all affliction. Affliction is subsumed in the crucifixion and made complete because here the unity between people and Jesus and Jesus with the Father is also completed as, again, Julian makes clear throughout chapters 21, 22 and 51. As Mona Logarbo contends:

> salvation for Julian is the restoration to and participation in this [completion] which unites and gives being to all reality and is revealed most comprehensively in Christ's Passion. To be restored to love and to participate in it is … to love others with the love which is at the heart of Christ's Passion. Indeed, *Christ's own pain and compassion is the basis of all human compassion.*[8]

---

5. Lamm, 'Revelation as Exposure', p. 63.

6. Julian, *Revelations*, 22:3, p. 66.

7. Julian, *Revelations*, 21:1, p. 63.

8. Mona Logarbo, 'Salvation Theology in Julian of Norwich: Sin, Forgiveness and Redemption in the *Revelations*', *Thought*, 61 (1986), p. 375; my emphasis added.

Julian's devotion to Christ's passion encourages people to seek consolation for their own suffering by reflecting upon his greater suffering and there experience his compassionate presence. As Anastasia Foyle writes, meditation on the cross strengthens people to 'perform acts of mercy to victims of suffering as devotion to the wounds of Christ'.[9]

Meditation on the passion powerfully conveys a sense of Jesus' solidarity in all forms of affliction. It consoles us and has at least the potential to carry us through our suffering even when we are least aware of it. It can heal in radically unexpected ways too.[10] Julian's image of kenotic love shining in the face of the dying Jesus is an expression of a loving God's response to the human condition and its suffering. It is a means of defeating our desolation when encircled by evil and undergoing the effects of destructive suffering.

Julian's Eschatology

The previous section dealt with Julian's reflections on the suffering Jesus and how these might provide hope and a process of unexpected healing for those who suffer affliction. It showed how this might come about when suffering people open themselves to the nearness of his divine presence, hard though that is to do. This section will consider the eschatological dimensions of that openness and divine presence and show how they too may be another hope-filled response to the problem of evil and destructive suffering. It will explore how Julian's eschatological approaches to theodicy have theological significance in the integration of theoretical and pastoral theodicies.

In an earlier chapter I briefly explored the eschatological responses to destructive suffering in the theodicies of John Hick and Michael Stoeber, both of whom attempt to provide coherent approaches to the afterlife and a hope for *post-mortem* opportunities for spiritual maturation. Their theodicies are about 'soul-making'. Both argue that abstract speculation on the afterlife may be a possible response to the problem of evil insofar as and in the degree to which it provides for healing, continued spiritual integration and transformation. I argued that, while their positions might be fully consistent with the idea of the God of Love, it is difficult to see how abstract speculation on the afterlife can bring about practical pastoral care without first positing the existence of some transitional, intermediate, state between the two.

---

9. Foyle, 'Human and Divine Suffering', paragraph 33.
10. Stoeber, *Reclaiming Theodicy*, pp. 50-51.

While Julian does not write of an intermediate state either, the eschatological dimensions of *Revelations* provides both a theoretical theological and a pastoral response to the problem of evil. As I have already argued, Julian deals with suffering and evil through the presence of divine compassion which constantly streams from the cross of Jesus. I have also argued that, for Julian, this bleeding, suffering, love conveys a solidarity with suffering people which transforms suffering and evil from the inside, without the need to justify them. The awareness of this brings comfort if not joy. Julian's approach to divine compassion has a strong pastoral emphasis that allows us to hope in the ordinary and Moltmannian sense of the word.

In her visions Julian received a locution from Jesus that 'It was necessary that there should be sin, but all shall be well, and all shall be well, and all manner of thing shall be well.'[11] This is the most quoted, abused and most misunderstood passage in the entire Julian opus. It is trotted out again and again as a panacea not only for when we truly suffer but also when we are just mildly down in the dumps. This simply will not do, especially in the context of considering the problem of evil. It is important to spend a while understanding what this locution properly means.

Julian is perplexed. All her life she has accepted the teaching of the Church that some people will live with God in some afterlife while the great majority of people will be eternally damned to hell. And yet the Christian faith demands that we dare to hope that all will be saved.[12] Why should we automatically assume that we will be among the blessed and not the damned? Julian's perplexity deepened when she was also told of the 'great deed' that God would perform during the last day:

> This is that great deed ordained by our Lord God from without beginning, treasured and hidden in is blessed breast, only known to himself; through this deed he shall make all things well. For like as the blessed Trinity made all things out of nought, right so the same blessed Trinity shall make well all that is not well.[13]

---

11. Julian, *Revelations*, 27:1, p. 81.

12. On this see esp. Hans Urs von Balthasar, *Dare we Hope that All Men Be Saved?* 2nd edition with *A Short Discourse on Hell* (San Francisco: Ignatius Press, 2004) and variously in his 5-volume *Theo-Drama,* esp. Vol. 3, tr. Graham Harrison (San Francisco: Ignatius Press, 1998). In addition see David Bentley Hart, *That All Shall Be Saved: Heaven, Hell and Universal Salvation* (New Haven and London: Yale University Press, 2019).

13. Julian, *Revelations*, 32:2, p. 93.

Julian sees, as we must see, that taken together these locutions do not promise that all shall be well *now*, but in the eschaton – *and nowhere else.* They assuage the effects of destructive suffering and evil now if, but only if, we look to the future which for Julian has only just begun. But they do rid us of all present and future fear of hell because, since God is wholly and entirely a God of Love in whom there is no anger at all, there can be no such thing. This surely explains why Julian was denied a vision of purgatory and hell.

Augustine of Hippo believed that scripture identifies a predestination to hell for most people, for only thus could the justice of God be vindicated. In *De Civitate Dei*[14] he gave intricate details of the destinies of the blessed and the damned. Writing from a somewhat right-wing evangelical perspective which has 'true piety' at its centre, Graham Keith claims that this is evidence of Augustine's pastoral concerns:

> [Augustine] believed that the fear of hell … helped many to take the first step toward true piety. Moreover, he believed that a diminished doctrine of Hell brought diminished standards of piety and a false hope within the Church … there was no hope that anyone who died impenitent or unbaptised could improve their standing after death.[15]

'True piety', whatever that may be, was (and is?) sought not for its own sake but because it is coerced through fear of damnation.

My reading of *De Civitate Dei* is somewhat different. It is one in which Augustine's concern has much less to do with predestination and much more to do with his view that all sin, especially so-called 'original sin', is a horrendous evil because it denies the loving goodness of God and deliberately separates us from it. The evil of sin intentionally sows the seeds of our destruction.

Again, whereas Keith sees Augustine as rejecting Origen's teaching[16] on divine punishment for sin as being corrective (thus giving hope after it) I regard Augustine as having accepted it, at least in part. Our positions then could not be more dissimilar. Origen taught that the possibility

---

14. St Augustine of Hippo, *De Civitate Dei*. www.documentacathilicaomnia (last accessed 14 July 2021).

15. Graham Keith, 'Patristic Views on Hell. Part 2', *Evangelical Quarterly*, Vol. 71, issue 4 (1999), pp. 297 and 299.

16. For more on Origen's teaching on sin, suffering, and evil see https://www.iep.utm.edu (last accessed 14 July 2021).

of repentance and reformation is implicit in all punishment. If divine punishment exists then, for Origen, it must cleanse human souls in such a way as they come to see that chastisement was for their own good and not, as Keith seems to think, an awareness of their eternal damnation. This rather school-masterly view was, I think, derived from Origen's understanding of the nature of God, namely, that divine punishment had to be good if it was to be just. The only purpose in divine punishment is not to condemn (John 3:17) but to draw all things to himself (John 12:32).

Despite my differences from Keith he is right in his assessment that his reading of Augustine prevailed in many 'Doom Paintings'[17] and preaching, described by Kelly James Clark in this way:

> The problem of God and Hell addressed by the medievals is the problem of justifying God's goodness while God permits or inflicts intense pain and suffering for eternity. The immediacy and duration of the pain and suffering are often justified by God's retributive justice: the damned, because of their *ante mortem* sins merit this sort of punishment.[18]

This is the sadistic God identified by contemporary pastoral theodicists as an inevitable component of theoretical theodicy.

The extent to which Julian was influenced by Augustinian theology is a matter of debate but it is clear that she rejected all these prevailing images. People are forgiven through the mercy which is divine love and it is this that assures her that 'all will be well' and that the 'great deed' will be benign not attritional.

If, as I and Joan Nuth believe, Julian's theology hints at a universal salvation (*apocatastasis*) then this is another reason for her to contradict and reject the blessed/damned duality. Julian does not teach a doctrine of universal salvation in a precise sense but she does come very close to doing so. The possibility is positioned in her belief that the human freedom to sin is never powerful enough to overcome God's salvific work in the passion and crucifixion of Jesus. Indeed, it may be the other way about. That is, Julian's soteriology can be situated in the concept of *apocatastasis* because the locution that 'all will be well' indicates the

---

17. Roger Rosewall, *Medieval Wall Paintings in English and Welsh Churches* (Woodbridge: Boydell Press, 2016).

18. Kelly James Clark, 'God is Great, God is Good: Medieval Conceptions of Divine Goodness and the Problem of Hell', *Religious Studies,* 37, issue 1 (2001), p. 16.

all-inclusive nature of God's desire for the final status of human life. This is especially the case if *apocatastasis* is one of those things spoken of at Matthew 19:26:

> Since God's love is infinitely more powerful than diabolic or human efforts to perpetuate evil, we can hope that God will effect the salvation even of those whom human judgement deems irrevocably lost. … Julian expresses faith in some eschatological deed, presently beyond human knowledge or understanding, through which God will bring *everything* into the fulfilment established as God's will from the beginning.[19]

Just as Julian's understanding that 'all will be well' does not apply yet but only in the eschaton, so it is not some naive optimism. Julian was deeply aware of human sin and its effects but insisted that they were too weak and frail to conquer our created goodness or God's Wisdom. People are, after all, created in the image of God (Gen. 1:27) and thus we can know the basis of our significance in the universe.[20] Julian's *Revelations* presents the image of a God who loves everything in an absolute way. Eschatological hope pertains to people who trust that divine love brings everything and everyone to eternal fulfilment.

I find further hints that Julian may have been a covert universalist in her calling into question *Unam Sanctum*[21] (= One God, one faith, one spiritual authority – the papal bull of 1302) and its axiom *extra ecclesiam nulla salus est* (= outside/beyond the Church there is no salvation) and with it the idea that salvation is reserved only for the baptised.[22] Nuth rightly points out that Julian nowhere finds this incompatible with the message of her visions or with scripture.[23] In my view the concept of the 'great deed' would itself be secure grounds for confronting the exclusivity of the axiom. The 'great deed' may turn out to be the unexpected salvation of those outside Christianity who do not meet either the historic or current requirements for salvation. If so, then all concepts of predestination,

---

19. Joan M. Nuth, *Wisdom's Daughter: The Theology of Julian of Norwich* (New York: Crossroad, 1991), p. 168; my emphasis added.
20. For more on this see the Institute for Faith, Work and Economics. www. tifwe.org/made-in-the-image-of-God-the-basis-of-our-significance (last accessed 14 July 2021).
21. See www.papalencyclicals.net (last accessed 14 July 2021).
22. For more on this doctrine and its subsequent impact on Western theology see Francis A Sullivan, *Salvation Outside the Church? Tracing the History of the Catholic Response* (New York: Paulist Press, 1992).
23. JNuth, *Wisdom's Daughter*, p. 165.

whether double or single, are irrelevant.[24] It calls into question traditional concepts of hell too.

Julian affirms the human culpability for sin even though it is 'no-thing'; 'And therefore it is God's will that we know what sin is, and pray earnestly and work diligently and humbly seek teaching so that we do not fall blindly into a state of sin; and if we do fall rise again quickly. For the soul can know no worse pain than to turn away from God at any time as a result of sin.'[25]

Knowledge of and culpability for sin lies only in the lowest part of our human nature, which is creaturely, not in the higher part of our being, which is more open to 'godly will': 'For in every soul … is a godly will that never assented to sin, nor ever shall. In the same way as there is a fleshly will in the lower part that may desire nothing good there is also a divine spark in the higher part, and this is so good that it may never desire evil but only good.'[26]

The soul is united to God in its being. God is united to our soul and bodies by having become human-stuff (*sarx*) for our redemption in the incarnation and this is continued in every consecration of every Eucharist every day. The Son of God who perfectly fulfils the 'godly will' of the Trinity resides in our souls for our salvation.[27]

For Julian this is the most beautiful and profound thought – and it is. The most eminent thing which God created is our soul which is nothing less than a hypostatic union of people with Christ. Through this hypostasis we are eternally 'knit' into the Father, who is the source and sanctification of all that will be saved.[28]

Julian asks, in what sense then does 'mortal sin' remain and points to the huge disparity between our judgement of ourselves and how God looks on us with pity not with blame:

> And therefore it often seems to us that we are in peril of death,
> half in Hell as it may be, because of the sorrow and the grief
> that sin has led us into. And thus we are closed off for the time

---

24. On the differences and their impact on the theodicic problem see Elijah Dubec, 'Predestination: Asymmetry of Good and Evil', *Dominica*. www.dominicanajournal.org (last accessed 14 July 2021).

25. Julian, *Revelations*, 76:2, p. 222.

26. Julian, *Revelations*, 37:2, p. 105.

27. Judith Lang, 'The Godly Wylle in Julian of Norwich', *Downside Review*, Vol. 102 (1984), p. 168.

28. John P.H. Clark, 'Predestination in Christ According to Julian of Norwich', *Downside Review*, Vol. 100, issue 389 (April 1982), p. 87.

being from the very sight of our blessed life. But at the same
time I saw steadfastly that we are not dead in the sight of God,
nor does he ever abandon us.[29]

Julian believes that we are incapable of ultimate defection from God
(and he with us because of the 'godly will' in our souls). Judith Lang
makes this clear: 'The redeeming sacrifice of Christ is the well-spring of
God's mercy, by which the constant failings of every soul … are forgiven,
and a promise made that there will be no final condemnation of sin in
that soul because of its eternally ordained union with God.'[30]

Julian's eschatology is fully consistent with the idea of a God of infinite
love and power. It provides a theoretical and pastoral response to the
theodicic problem and potentially consoles those who are overwhelmed
by suffering. Through her theme of divine compassion she allows us to
hope for healing from the destructive effects of suffering. This compassion
initially appears embedded in the crucifixion, and subsequently flowing
out into eschatological speculation. Both are enlarged by her complete
refusal to accept that there is any anger in God who demands retributive
justice by sending people to burn in the fires of hell. Instead, she offers
a teleological and eschatological view of theodicy in which evil and
suffering are, for the moment, instruments of God's will. They are limited
and finite, not eternal for they have no substantive existence.

In short, Julian's eschatological view that 'all will be well' at the end
of time provides hope. It opposes all notions of a God of anger. God *is*
love (1 John 4:7-21). He created us in love. He holds us in love and will
preserve us in love now and forever.

It is in this way, I contend, that Julian offers one possible means of
(re)integrating the theoretical and pastoral approaches to the problem
of evil.

Towards a Julian Theodicy

As I explained in an earlier chapter there is a tendency in modern
theology to abandon theoretical approaches to theodicy in favour
of entirely pastoral ones, because theoretical theodicies are believed
not only to provide inadequate answers to the problem of evil but to
perpetuate it. Here I will emphasise the support which a close reading of
Revelations of Divine Love gives to theoretical theodicy and at the same

---

29. Julian, *Revelations*, 72:2, p. 210.
30. Lang, 'Godly Wylle', p. 172.

time it is useful to pastoral theodicists in providing a defence of their approach on a cognitive level. In this way, I will argue, Julian's theodicy reintegrates both approaches.

Julian had been told that evil and suffering are the result of and punishment for sin. God's love was left out of the account. Julian struggled with that even in the midst of the well recorded and exhaustively examined sufferings of her day. It did not and does not seem compatible with a loving God: 'For some of us believe that God is almighty and may do everything; and that he is all wisdom and is able to do everything; but that he is love and determined to do everything, at that point we stop short.'[31]

It is always easier to control and punish than to love. God's love is constant and cannot be quenched (Song of Solomon 8:7) but people blind themselves to it and the Church shamefully contributes to that blindness. People no longer believe they are loved. Worse still they do not believe they are deserving of it and this takes us to the brink of hell.[32] Yet we *are always* deserving of it.[33]

Julian was a compassionate and intelligent theologian, the equal of if not surpassing the greatest thinkers of her age, including Aquinas,[34] because of her use of natural reason. Julian's willingness to tease out as many meanings as possible from her parable of the Lord and the Servant is evidence of this. The meanings enabled her to find a theoretical theological way to support the pastoral theodicy immediately achieved in her visions. Through natural reason, Julian sought a more rational answer to her basic question of how all things shall be well given the agony of the world. In the conclusion to the Long Text she says that it is all a matter of unending love.

Julian was not content with a simple soothing for suffering. She wanted to understand and concluded that evil and suffering are compatible with divine omnipotence and omniscience, but only through the nature of divine love as shown in her visions.

Julian's transition from pastoral to theoretical theodicy comes about because of her understanding that a philosophical response is always required at the end of any theodicy. After all, the owl of Minerva flies only in the evening.[35] By allowing the owl its wings, Julian demonstrates

---

31. Julian, *Revelations*, 73:4, p. 214.
32. Julian, *Revelations,* 39:1.
33. Julian, *Revelations*, 50.
34. Turner, *Julian of Norwich*. See also his *Thomas Aquinas: A Portrait*.
35. G.W. Hegel, *Elements of the Philosophy of Right*, ed. Allen W. Wood, tr. H.B. Nisbet (Cambridge: CUP, 1991).

that theoretical theodicies can equally be regarded as a practical response to suffering. Theory is its own form of praxis and to say this is not always the philosophical illusion that Harcourt believes it to be.[36]

If for some, Julian's position is a little too optimistic in the face of horrendous evils, it is easily explained by her overwhelming joy in the goodness of God. Reynolds argues that this is by no means astonishing even in the circumstances of the late fourteenth century.[37] God does not blame us. The relationship between people and God is never broken by failure.[38] Julian affirms the truth that Jesus is the manifestation of divinity to people and the manifestation of people to God, despite our weakness.[39] Patricia Vinje says that Julian's optimistic joy in *Revelations* makes Julian a 'herald of hope in the face of social and religious depression'[40] because of her solidarity in love, to which I would add that to speak of Mother-Christ is to affirm that the *logos* became human incorporating all humanity in itself. This is the unbreakable bond and the reason why God has no anger.

This hopeful bond is entirely parallel to the eschatological direction of modern systematic theology since the 1970s. 'With a gratitude based on God's fidelity ... the Christian can look back, knowing that God, who has so wonderfully begun his work in creation, is pursuing it in an ineffable way in Jesus ... and will fulfil it in him on the day of the Parousia.'[41]

Julian's eschatological hope flows from her conviction that everything, including evil and suffering, is in God's hands. God has the power to make all things (eventually) well and on this basis offers an example of how to trust even in the midst of the disconnection of desolation and despair. As I have insisted, and need to repeat, this is not a polyanna-ish view but one entirely relevant to the substantive circumstances of today's all-too-hurting world.

---

36. Bernard E. Harcourt, *Critique and Praxis: A Critical Philosophy of Illusions, Values and Actions* (New York: Columbia University Press, 2020).

37. Anna Maria Reynolds, 'Julian of Norwich: Woman of Hope', *Mystics Quarterly*, Vol. 10, issue 3 (1984), pp. 118-19.

38. Anna Maria Reynolds, 'Woman of Hope', in Robert Llewelyn (ed.), *Julian Woman of our Day* (London: Darton Longman & Todd, 1985)., pp. 15-16.

39. Reynolds, 'Woman of Hope', p. 17.

40. Patricia Mary Vinje, *An Understanding of Love According to the Anchoress Julian of Norwich* (Salzburg: Institut für Anglistik und Amerikanistik, 1983), pp. 40-41.

41. Bernard Haring, *Hope is the Remedy* (Garden City, NY: Doubleday, 1972), p. 145.

Julian demonstrates that theoretical theodicy, as a cognitive-level response to evil and suffering, may equally be regarded as operating on a practical and pastoral level as it generates consolation and hope. Thus her theoretical theodicy is *not* itself a source or cause of evil. Rather, her optimistic eschatology offers not only the possibility of hope and healing but provides the motivation to effectively respond to existential dilemmas (that are also intellectual) without the need to abandon theoretical theodicy.

It remains to be explored how, in other ways, Julian's theodicy integrated theoretical and pastoral approaches and this will occupy us for the remainder of this chapter. Julian sets out her method of integration in chapter 80 of *Revelations*. It consists of three aspects of the same whole: natural reason, the teachings of the Church and divine grace.

> By three things in this life does a man stand; by the same three God is worshipped, and we are helped onwards, kept and saved. The first is the use of … natural reason; the second is the common teaching of Holy Church; the third is the inward work of Grace by the Holy Spirit. And these three all come from the one God: God is the ground of our natural reason; and God is the basis for the teaching of Holy Church; and God himself is the Holy Spirit. And these three are all distinct gifts and he wills that we treasure them and give close attention to them. For they are all continually at work within us; and they are of great importance. His will is that we know something of their great importance – an ABC as it were – but we shall know all we need to know in heaven. And that is to encourage us.[42]

This is none other than the search for faith in our common life. Julian's theology is never far from that. The learning that comes from daily life and our religious experience cannot be separated. Julian's own 'experience' did not consist of perpetual visions and locutions. It consisted far more in an awareness and practice of the presence of God with her moment by moment and this impelled her to give counsel to those behind the curtain of the street window of her cell. In our response to that same love we too are able to meet people in their crises. Moreover, it is 'both the basis from which we better understand doctrine, and a

---

42. Julian, *Revelations*, 80:1, p. 231.

practical consequence of that understanding as we discover in our daily lives the truth of God's love and delight'.[43]

The extent to which this is or is not evidence of Julian's knowledge and experience of monastic spirituality may be hotly debated, but it does not concern us here. For our purposes it is essential to recognise that it is living in correspondence with divine love that makes for the proper use of natural reason and Church teaching. For Julian both are adjusted by divine grace as revealed in the passion of Christ. It is grace that unifies the other two and all other aspects of her life and thought. It utterly transforms some traditional doctrines: the Last Things[44] and the nature of Salvation among them.

Julian is not only interested in reconciling sinfulness with faith, but in reconciling suffering with a God who is nothing but love. Where these pairs seem to contradict each other she uses a carefully repeated application of critical distinctions to attempt to harmonise the dissonances. Her *theologia crucis* and eschatology have positive impacts on contemporary theodicy because they urge us to rethink our understandings of destructive sufferings by completely rejecting the claim that it is the consequence of and punishment for sin. Far less does it demand that we posit a form of retributive justice or atonement by substitution.

Julian does not forget the innocent victims of evil and suffering either. She compassionately responds to them and questions the supposed inevitability of further suffering the pains of hell as retributive justice applied for 'original' and personal sin. Julian replaces these ideas with a strong teleological and eschatological framework in which all suffering will be overcome by divine love.

Julian also rejects the view held by some contemporary pastoral theodicists that theoretical theodicy is entirely incapable of offering hope and healing to suffering people. The passion and the cross of Jesus provide a profound sense of empathy and solidarity with them in their afflictions and this becomes a lived religious experience of divine consolation and presence. Moreover, Julian's hope that 'all shall be well' and her confidence that all will be saved in the 'great deed' at the end of time pertains to people who, even in their suffering, can trust that divine love can and will bring everything, especially evil and suffering, to an

---

43. Jantzen, *Julian of Norwich*, p. 105.

44. For a comprehensive survey of how the Last Things were understood by medieval people see Caroline Walker Bynum and Paul Freedman (eds.), *Last Things: Death and the Apocalypse in the Middle Ages* (Philadephia: University of Pennsylvania Press, 2000).

eternal fulfilment. Julian's eschatology provides hope for the possibility of healing for suffering people – including those whose suffering is made worse by forms of Christianity that are obsessed with sin and punishment, in her day and ours.

Contemporary theodicists would do well to pay close attention to Julian's paradigm shift away from the God of anger towards God as Being-itself who is divine love by way of identity and not predication. This is clearly seen in her belief that divine compassion is revealed in the resurrection event. The resurrection and the eschatological dimensions which flow from it have a strong pastoral orientation that offers hope for healing and recovery from the effects of all evils and suffering. I maintain that, if we take the two together, we come to recognise that Julian's theodicy proffers a positive integration of both the theoretical and pastoral approaches to the problem of evil.

Another important example of this is to be found in Julian's reworking of the interconnections between gender, the body and sin. Her reworking ensures that the response to the problem of evil can never encourage theological or ideological distortions of suffering which have been identified by some pastoral critiques of theoretical theodicy. As I argued in a previous chapter, Julian's theology overcomes the supposed supremacy of soul over body. For her, people are an insoluble unity of both. Hence in her *Power, Gender and Christian Mysticism,* Grace Jantzen persuasively argued that Julian's theology has an embodied spirituality at its core that 'brings the whole self, sensuality included, into the unity of the love of God'.[45]

Julian fragments the negative associations of women with the body, the so-called 'Fall' and sin. The associations were (and are) oppressive tools that caused much suffering for women – a destructive suffering deliberately and socially constructed in the Christian tradition. In contrast, Julian values the body and defines sin in ways that do not implicate sexuality as bearing the penalty for sin or women as being more responsible for sin than men. Hence, Julian avoids many of the criticisms that some pastoral theodicists lodge against some themes in theoretical theodicy. Julian's interconnections provide a compelling theoretical framework for her pastoral concerns, which also contributes to the contemporary discussions concerning the possible relationship between explicitly theoretical and pastoral themes in constructing a reasonable and useful theodicy.

---

45. Jantzen, *Power, Gender and Christian Mysticism*, p. 149.

Any theodicy based on Julian's theology and spirituality must therefore provide persuasive examples of integration of theoretical and pastoral approaches to the problem of evil. It must, like Julian herself, be capable of unravelling emotional tangles and intellectual perplexities. It must allow for paradox while seeking resolutions of each of these in the larger framework of authentic Christian doctrine and the magisterium. If it cannot or will not do this it is difficult to see how we can even begin to pose or attempt to answer the problem of evil in the twenty-first century.

Conclusion

This book has focussed on the theology of Julian of Norwich in specific ways which might show us how, why and in what ways it may make a positive contribution to the construction of an adequate answer to the problem of evil in the twenty-first century. It has discussed the often bitter and unresolved divide between contemporary theodicists who take a pastoral approach to the problem and those whose writings seem to be purely theoretical. I have argued that, while Julian's theology and spirituality can never heal the entrenched divides, it can at least be regarded as a useful resource for both sides because it can make positive contributions to their positions.

Julian's *Revelations of Divine Love* are the product of her theological creativity. It is a dynamic that exists between her mystical experience and her theology. If we are to use Julian's theology now we must first recognise that both aspects – mystical experience and theological endeavour – inseparably intertwine in a single skein. When Julian deals with the emotions of depression and despair she does so in ways that allow her to question God. She questions the nature of divine power and benevolence, the origin and nature of sin, the meaning of judgement and punishment. Above all, like all good theodicy, she attempts to reconcile the daily experience of evil and suffering with faith in an all-knowing, all-loving God.

One of the key reasons for Julian writing *Revelations* was to interpret her mystical visions in an intelligible narrative of divine love which, she hoped, would comfort her fellow Christians as they faced devastation. There was a lot of devastation to be had in late fourteenth-century England. Her theology is deeply pastoral in this respect but only in a way in which she involves herself theoretically with resolving what she sees as the ever-vexing problems of sin and providence. Julian achieves this remarkable synthesis by honouring the truth of her mystical experiences and combining it with the use of her natural reason and the authentic doctrines of the Church. This is the contact point that offers enormous further significance and implications for contemporary theodicy.

Even so, Julian was greatly troubled, as we should be troubled, by accepted theologies of divine anger, retribution, punishment and demands for atonement by substitution. Without ever denying human sin and its seriousness she utterly rejected these concepts as adding more fuel to an already cruel fire which, unlike that of Newman's Gerontius,[1] burns but cannot transform. Julian's pivotal insight here is the distinction between human and divine perspectives through which she arrives at a new understanding to explain sin and evil in the light of divine love. When viewed from a divine perspective, revealed in her visions, sin has no place. It is no-thing. It has no being either now or eternally. It cannot thwart God's loving intentions towards all that he has made.

In her parable of the Lord and the Servant, Julian realised that the original transgression of human beings was *not* deliberate and wilful rebellion, but rather an inadvertent separation from God. The God of the parable looks with pity not with blame, for in him is no anger at all.

The most pressing issue for Julian, as it is in all systematic theodicies, was how to comprehend the nature of God while recognising that God is not only all-knowing and all-powerful, but all-loving. Julian regards sin, suffering and evil from an eschatological point of view and explores their functions in divine providence. Her theology is teleological. It focusses on the purposes and ends of evil. She does not take an aetiological approach concerned with the causes and consequences of it. This stands in stark contrast to the juridical paradigm in the Christian response to the theodicic problem. Retribution always conflicts with Christian hope, but cannot overcome it.

Julian's understanding of the nature of God is bound up with her understanding of what human beings are and what they do. She values the body, including its sensuality and sexuality, and this provides inter-esting and fruitful underpinnings for contemporary pastoral theodicy. For Julian the body is sacred and as such must be regarded as being inviolate. It is sacred because our bodies are consubstantial with the human body of Jesus who, in his divine nature was, as we affirm in the Creed, consubstantial with the Father. On this view, individual Christians become a little Christ and the icon of Christ to the world – demanding as much respect as we would give to him. It is this, as Julian

---

1. John Henry Newman, *The Dream of Gerontius*. www.newmanreader.org (last accessed July 2021).

put it, that makes us Jesus' dear-worthy friends. The body is cherished and enfolded in the all-encompassing love of God, as we see in Julian's image of Mother-Christ.

Julian uses the image of Christ's Motherhood to reveal the unbreakable bond between God and people. It is from this unity that she concludes that God is never angry and can never be. Anger is simply not part of the divine make up. This is a key Christological insight and contributes much to our understanding of the trope of Mother-Christ both in Revelations and elsewhere in medieval theology – and especially as the feminine was increasingly devalued in later thinking as Jenny Bledsoe has usefully pointed out.[2]

The feminine is central to Julian's attempts to come to terms with the problem of evil and suffering, seeing in it overwhelming compassion for all victims wherever and whatever they suffer. There can be no resolution to the theodicic problem without compassion, co-suffering. We suffer alongside those who suffer because Jesus first suffered alongside us in his passion and death. Our pain is reflected in and taken up into his pain. His sharing of human suffering makes explicit that relationship in love between God and people. Julian's powerful, graphic and at times somewhat gruesome images of the suffering of Jesus convey that solidarity.

Julian's Christological approach to theodicy may, I think, be unique in medieval writings, certainly in England. It need hardly be said that this is quite different from the compassion found in the cult of the Virgin Mary in the same period, although an internet search under the terms 'Mother-Christ in Medieval Theology' confuses the two for at least the first four pages of results. An explicitly Christological approach to the problem of evil is far from common in much modern theologising too. It is, above all, her Christological approach, her image of the compassionate God, that gives her the confidence that all will be well. This, as we have seen repeatedly, is an eschatological hope and it is one which is entirely relevant in our world of no hope, in which we face all manner of external threats and internal fears, in a world where many are, like the holy souls in purgatory, allowed to 'suffer on'[3] because that is, apparently but shamefully, just how things are.

---

2. Jenny Bledsoe, 'Feminine Images of Jesus; Later Medieval Christology and the Devaluation of the Feminine', *Intermountain West Journal of Religious Studies*, Vol. 3, issue 1, article 4 (2001), pp. 33-59.

3. John Henry Newman, 'Hymn for the Holy Souls', 1857. www.catholic.org /prayers (last accessed July 2021).

Julian does not solve the problem of evil. No one can, however systematic their theology and philosophy might be and however practically engaged their pastoral care may be too. To do so is *not* Julian's concern. As this book has shown, her primary task was to explore the nature of divine love in relation to evil, sin and suffering and to examine how her own mystical experiences and theological reflection upon them might make a positive contribution to it. It was this that equipped her with the unique theological and pastoral insight for finding an adequate, though always partial, response to evil and suffering. Her effort to, as it were, 'vindicate' the loving care of God in this context provides psychological, emotional, theological, spiritual and practical consolation. It offers hope at a time of no hope and in this way makes a positive contribution to contemporary debates between theoretical and pastoral theodicists.

There are a number of other issues which an examination of Julian of Norwich and the problem of evil reveals which cannot be explored here but which would reward further study. For example, there is the question of how freedom of thought and action is impaired by evil and horrendous suffering and whether, given this impairment, it is still reasonable for Christians to endeavour to create the conditions under which the final kingdom of God might be established on earth as they already are in heaven. In other words, is this *really* the best of all possible worlds? Since all evidence would suggest that it is not, maybe we should look for and build another one?

I have left entirely out of my account what Julian might have to say about natural evil and how this might impact on our understandings of our current pressing concerns such as climate change.

Then there is the whole question of purgatory and hell. This is important if we are to understand Julian's theology, and possible radicality, in the context of the fourteenth-century English Church if not in ours. If, as I believe, Julian had at least some sympathy with the concept of universal salvation then such an exploration might be very interesting indeed, even if, in the end, we come to the conclusion that purgatory and hell fall away in the light of God's great deed of 'oneing' everything and everyone with himself.

There is also much valuable academic work to be done, I think, as to what Julian might have to tell us about institutional evils and structural sins. It would be interesting to explore in more detail how her *theologia crucis* might provide deeper insights into this problem

Despite these omissions this book has argued that as a woman and as a mystic Julian of Norwich makes a positive contribution to debates in modern theodicy. It has shown that Julian's understanding of the nature of God (as pure love) illustrates how he is actively involved with individuals living in destructive circumstances. It has argued that her mystical theology goes far beyond the limits and scope of a non-mystical theology in the matter of theodicy.

Finally, this book has argued that Julian's *Revelation of Divine Love* is a useful resource for all those concerned with the problem of evil. It should be read, studied, analysed and used as such. It will not resolve the theodicic problem but it may resolve the sad divisions between theologians who try to do so and reintegrate their approaches into a cogent analysis as to why evil and suffering are, or are not, compatible with an all-knowing, all-powerful but all-loving God.

Above all, this book has argued that by using Julian's reflections on the problem of evil we can ensure that all contemporary theodicy can be utterly sensitive to the lived experience of suffering and evil. We can only do so if we insist with Julian that God IS Love and as such actively involved in our pains, moment by moment, no matter what.

Bibliography

Julian of Norwich: Editions of *Revelations of Divine Love*

Julian of Norwich: Showing of Love, tr. Julia Bolton-Holloway (Collegeville, MN: The Liturgical Press, 2003)

Julian of Norwich: Showings, ed. and tr. Edmund College and James Walsh. Classics of Western Spirituality (New York: Paulist Press, 1978)

Julian of Norwich: A Showing of God's Love. The Shorter Version of Sixteen Revelations of Divine Love, ed. Anna Maria Reynolds. Inner Life Series (London: Longmans Green & Co., 1958)

Revelations of Divine Love Julian of Norwich, tr. Grace Warwick, modernised by Yolande Clark, with an Introduction by A. N. Wilson (London: SPCK, 2017)

Julian of Norwich and Theodicy

Anselm, *Saint Anselm: Basic Writings,* tr. S.N. Dean (La Salle, IL: Open Court, 1979)

Aulen, Gustaf, *Christus Victor* (London: SPCK, 1978)

Beilby, James and Paul R. Eddy (eds.), *The Nature of Atonement* (Downers Grove, IL: Inter-Varsity Press, 2006)

Boserma, Hans, *Violence, Hospitality and the Cross: Reappropriating the Atonement Tradition* (Grand Rapids, MI: Baker Academic, 2004)

Bynum, Caroline Walker, *Fragmentation and Redemption: Essays on Gender and the Human Body in Medieval Religion* (New York: Zone Books, 1992)

Bynum, Caroline Walker, *Holy Feast, Holy Fast: The Religious Significance of Food for Medieval Women* (Berkeley, CA: University of California Press, 1987)

Bynum, Caroline Walker, *Jesus as Mother: Studies in the Spirituality of the High Middle Ages* (Berkeley, CA: University of California Press, 1982)

Bynum, Caroline Walker and Paul Freedman (eds.), *Last Things: Death and the Apocalypse in the Middle Ages* (Philadelphia: University of Pennsylvania Press, 2000)

Clark, Kelly James, 'God is Great, God is Good: Medieval Conceptions of Divine Goodness and the Problem of Hell', *Religious Studies,* Vol 37, issue 1 (March 2001), pp. 15-31

Fleming, William, *Arts, Music and Ideas* (New York: Holt, Rinehart & Winston Inc., 1970)

Fox, Thomas C., *Sexuality and Catholicism* (New York: George Brailler, 1995)

Genovesi, Vincent, *In Pursuit of Love: Catholic Morality and Human Sexuality* (Collegeville, MN: The Liturgical Press, 1996)

Hall, M Elizabeth Lewis and Erik Thoennes Erik, 'At Home in Our Bodies: Implications of the Incarnation for Embodiment and Christian Higher Education', *Christian Scholars Review,* Vol. 36, issue 1 (2006), pp. 29-45

Haring, Bernard, *Hope is the Remedy* (Garden City, NY: Doubleday, 1972)

Jungling, Laurie A., 'Passionate Order: Order and Sexuality in Augustine's Theology', *Word and World – Theology for Christian Ministry,* Vol. 27 (Summer 2007), pp. 315-24

Keith, Graham, 'Patristic Views of Hell. Part 2', *Evangelical Quarterly,* Vol.71, issue 4 (1999), pp. 291-310

Kelly, David F., 'Sexuality and Concupiscence in Augustine', *Annual of the Society of Christian Ethics* (1983), pp. 83-116

Leclerq, Jean, *The Love of Learning and the Desire for God* (New York: Fordham University Press, 1961)

McNamer, Sarah, *Affective Meditation and the Invention of Medieval Compassion* (Philadelphia: University of Pennsylvania Press, 2010)

Nelson, James, *Between Two Gardens: Reflections on Spirituality and Religious Experience* (Cleveland, OH: The Pilgrim Press, 1983)

Nelson, James, *Embodiment: An Approach to Sexuality and Christian Theology* (Minneapolis: Augsburg Publishing House, 1978)

Norton, Richard, *How to See a Vision: Contemplative Ethics in Julian of Norwich and Teresa of Avila* (Bloomington, IN: AuthorHouse, 2013)

Norton, Richard, *Julian of Norwich: Apostle of Pain* (Bloomington, IN: AuthorHouse, 2020)

Norton, Richard, *Love IS His Meaning: Julian of Norwich and the Doctrine of Salvation* (Eugene, OR: Wipf & Stock, forthcoming)

Park, Andrew Sung, *From Hurt to Healing: A Theology of the Wounded* (Nashville, TN: Abingdon Press, 2004)

Park, Andrew Sung, *True Atonement: Christ's Healing for Sinners, Victims and the Whole Creation* (Louisville, KY: Westminster/John Knox Press, 2009)

Ranke-Heinemann, Uta, *Eunuchs for the Kingdom of Heaven: Women, Sexuality and the Catholic Church,* tr. Peter Heinegg (New York: Doubleday, 1990)

Ross, Ellen M., 'She Wept and She Cried Right Loud for Sorrow and For Pain: Suffering, the Spiritual Journey and Women's Experiences in Late Medieval Mysticism', in Ulrike Wiethaus (ed.), *Maps of Flesh and Light* (Syracuse, NYk: Syracuse University Press, 1993)

Ross, Ellen M., *The Grief of God: Images of the Suffering Jesus in Late Medieval England* (Oxford: Oxford University Press, 1997)

Ruether, Rosemary Radford, 'Augustine, Sexuality, Gender and Women', in Judith Stark (ed.), *Feminist Interpretations of Augustine* (University Park, PA: Pennsylvania State University Press, 2007), pp. 47-67

Ruether, Rosemary Radford, *Gaia and God: An Ecofeminist Theology of Earth Healing* (San Francisco: Harper San Francisco, 1992)

Ruether, Rosemary Radford, 'Misogynism and Virginal Feminism in the Fathers of the Church', in Rosemary Ruether (ed.), *Religion and Sexism: Images of Women in the Jewish and Christian Traditions* (New York: Simon & Schuster, 1974), pp. 150-83

Ruether, Rosemary Radford, 'Sex in the Catholic Tradition', in Lisa Isherwood (ed.), *The Good News of the Body: Sexuality and Feminism* (New York: New York University Press, 2000), pp. 35-53

Ruether, Rosemary Radford, *Sexism and God-Talk: Toward a Feminist Theology* (Boston: Beacon Press, 1993)

Sanders, John Ed, *Atonement and Violence* (Nashville, TN: Abingdon Press, 2006)

Sebastian, Joseph, *God as Feminine: A Dialogue* (Frankfurt am Main and New York: P. Lang, 1995)

Sia, Marian F. and Sia Santiago, *From Suffering to God: Exploring Our Image of God in the Light of Suffering* (New York: St Martin's Press, 1994)

Stark, Judith Chelius, 'Augustine and Women: In God's Image, But Less So', in Judith Stark (ed.), *Feminist Interpretations of Augustine* (University Park, PA: Pennsylvania State University Press, 2007)

Sullivan, Francis A., *A Salvation Outside the Church? Tracing the History of the Catholic Response* (New York: Paulist Press, 1992)

Tuchman, Barbara W., *A Distant Mirror: The Calamitous 14th Century* (New York: Ballatine Books, 1978)

Weaver, J. Denny, *The Non-Violent Atonement* (Grand Rapids, MI: William Eerdmans Publishing Co., 2001)

Julian of Norwich: Books, Articles and Other Writings

Abbot, Christopher, 'His Body, the Church: Julian of Norwich's Vision of Christ Crucified', *Downside Review*, Vol. 115, issue 398 (January 1997), pp. 1-22

Abbot, Christopher, *Julian of Norwich: Autobiography and Theology* (Cambridge: D.S. Brewer, 1999)

Adams, Marilyn McCord, 'Julian of Norwich on the Tender Loving Care of Mother Jesus', in Kelly James Clark (ed.), *Our Knowledge of God: Essays on Natural and Philosophical Theology* (Dordrecht: Kluwer Academic Publishers, 1992)

Aers, David and Lynn Stately, *The Power of the Holy: Religion Politics and Gender in Late Medieval Culture* (University Park, PA: Pennsylvania State University Press, 1996)

Ahlgren, Gillian T.W., 'Julian of Norwich's Theology of Eros', *Spiritus* (Spring 2005), pp. 37-53

Allchin, A.M., 'Julian of Norwich and the Continuity of Tradition', in Robert Llewelyn (ed.), *Julian: Woman of our Day* (London: Darton Longman & Todd, 1985)

Allen, Christine, 'Christ Our Mother in Julian of Norwich', *Studies in Religious Studies/Sciences Religieuses,* Vol. 10, issue 4 (1981), pp. 421-28

Baker, Denise Nowakowski, 'Julian of Norwich and Anchoritic Literature', *Mystics Quarterly,* Vol. 19, issue 4 (1993), pp. 148-60

Baker, Denise Nowakowski, *Julian of Norwich's Showings: From Vision to Book* (Princeton, NJ: Princeton University Press, 1994)

Baker, Denise Nowakowski, 'The Structure of the Soul and the Godly Wille in Julian of Norwich's Showings', in E. A. Jones (ed.), *The Medieval Mystical Tradition in England.* Exeter Symposium VII. Papers read at Charney Manor 2004 (Cambridge: D.S. Brewer, 2004), pp. 177-88

Barker, Paula S. Datso, 'The Motherhood of God in Julian of Norwich's Theology', *Downside Review,* Vol. 100 (1982), pp. 290-304

Bauerschmidt, Frederick C., *Julian of Norwich and the Mystical Body Politic of Christ* (Notre Dame, IN: Notre Dame University Press, 1999)

Bauerschmidt, Frederick C., 'Julian of Norwich Incorporated', *Modern Theology,* Vol. 13, issue 1 (January 1997), pp. 75-100

Bauerschmidt, Frederick C., 'Order, Freedom and Kindness: Julian of Norwich on the Edge of Modernity', *Theology Today,* Vol. 60 (2003), pp. 63-81

Bauerschmidt, Frederick C., 'Seeing Jesus: Julian of Norwich and the Text of Christ's Body', *Journal of Medieval and Early English Studies,* Vol. 27, issue 2 (1997), pp. 189-214

Beer, Francis, *Women and Mystical Experience in the Middle Ages* (Woodbridge and Rochester, NY: Boydell Press, 1992)

Bozak-DeLeon, Lillian, 'The Soteriology of Julian of Norwich', in John Apczynski (ed.), *Theology and the University* (Lanham, MD: University Press of America, 1990), pp. 37-46

Bradley, Ritamary, 'Julian of Norwich: Everyone's Mystic', in William F. Pollard and Robert Boenig (eds.), *Mysticism and Spirituality in Medieval England* (Woodbridge: Boydell & Brewer, 1997), pp. 139-58

Bradley, Ritamary, 'Julian of Norwich: Writer and Mystic', in Paul E Szarmach (ed.), *An Introduction to the Mystics of Medieval Europe: Fourteen Original Essays* (Albany, NY: State University of New York Press, 1984), pp. 195-216

Bradley, Ritamary, *Julian's Way: A Practical Commentary on Julian of Norwich* (London: Harper Collins Religious, 1992)

Bradley, Ritamary, 'Metaphors of Cloth and Clothing in the Showings of Julian of Norwich', *Medievalia: A Journal of Medieval Studies,* Vol. 9 (1986), pp. 269-82

Bradley, Ritamary, 'Motherhood Theme in Julian of Norwich', *Fourteenth Century Mystics Newsletter,* Vol. 2, issue 4 (1976), pp. 25-38

Bradley, Ritamary, 'Mysticism in the Motherhood of God Similitude of Julian of Norwich', *Studica Mystica*, Vol. 8 (1985), pp. 4-14

Bradley, Ritamary, 'Patristic Background of the Motherhood Similitude in Julian of Norwich', *Christian Scholars Review*, Vol. 8, issue 2 (1978), pp. 101-13

Bradley, Ritamary, 'Perceptions of Self in Julian of Norwich's Showings', *Downside Review*, Vol. 104 (1986), pp. 227-39

Branolino, Gina, 'The Chiefe and Principal Mene: Julian of Norwich's Redefining of the Body in *A Revelation of Love*', *Mystics Quarterly*, Vol. 22, issue 3 (September 1996), pp. 102-10

Cannon, Christopher, 'Enclosure', in Caroline Dinshaw and David Wallace (eds), *The Cambridge Companion to Medieval Women's Writing* (Cambridge: Cambridge University Press, 2003), pp. 109-23

Caspar, Ruth, 'All Shall Be Well: Prototypical Symbols of Hope', *Journal of the History of Ideas*, Vol. 42, issue 1 (1981), pp. 139-50

Chilson, Robert, *All Will Be Well* (Notre Dame, IN: Ave Maria Press, 1996)

Clark, John P.F., '*Fiducia* in Julian of Norwich I', *Downside Review*, Vol 99, issue 335 (1981), pp. 97-108

Clark, John P.F., '*Fiducia* in Julian of Norwich II', *Downside Review*, Vol. 99, issue 336 (1981), pp. 214-29

Clark, John P.F., 'Nature, Grace and the Trinity in Julian of Norwich', *Downside Review*, Vol. 100, issue 340 (1982), pp. 203-20

Clark, John P.F., 'Predestination in Christ According to Julian of Norwich', *Downside Review*, 100, issue 339 (April 1982), pp. 79-91

Clark, John P.F., 'Time and Eternity in Julian of Norwich', *Downside Review*, Vol. 109, issue 377 (1991), pp. 259-76

Conduct, David, *A Simpler Path - Julian of Norwich and Marcus Aurelius* ([Durham]: independently published, 2021)

Cummings, Charles, 'The Motherhood of God According to Julian of Norwich', in Lillian Thomas Shank and John A Nichols (eds.), *Medieval Religious Women*, Vol. 2: *Peaceweavers* (Kalamazoo, MI: Cistercian Publications, 1987), pp. 305-14

Dale, Judith, 'Sin is Behovenly – Art and Theodicy in Julian of Norwich', *Mystics Quarterly*, Vol. 25, issue 4 (December 1999), pp. 127-46

Dearborn, Kerry, 'The Crucified Christ as the Motherly God: The Theology of Julian of Norwich', *Scottish Journal of Theology*, Vol. 55 (2002), pp. 282-302

Del Maestro, Marguerite L., 'Julian of Norwich: Parables of the Lord and Servant Radical Orthodoxy', *Mystics Quarterly*, Vol. 14, issue 2 (June 1988), pp. 84-93

Donahue-White, Patricia, 'Reading Divine Maternity in Julian of Norwich', *Spiritus* (Spring 2005), pp. 19-36

Dreyer, Elizabeth A., 'The Trinitarian Theology of Julian of Norwich: Mysticism and Theology, a Test Case', *Studies in Spirituality*, Vol. 4 (1994), pp. 79-93

Eugen, Abram van, 'Shifting Perspectives: Sin and Salvation in Julian's *A Revelation of Divine Love*', *Literature and Theology*, Vol. 23, issue 1 (March 2009)

Fanning, Steven C., 'Mitigations of Fear of Hell and Purgatory in the Later Middle Ages: Julian of Norwich and Catherine of Genoa', in Anne Scott and Cynthia Kosso (eds.), *Fear and its Representations in the Middle Ages and Renaissance* (Turnhout: Brepols, 2002), pp. 295-310

Gatta, Julia, 'Julian of Norwich: Theology as Pastoral Art', *Anglican Theological Review,* Vol. 63, issue 2 (April 1981), pp. 173-81

Hagan, Susan K., 'The Visual Theology of Julian of Norwich', in Frank Willaert et al. (eds.), *Medieval Memory, Image and Text* (Turnhout: Brepols, 2004), pp. 145-60

Harries, Richard, 'On the Brink of Universalism', in Robert Llewelyn (ed.), *Julian - Woman of our Day* (London: Darton Longman & Todd, 1985), pp. 41-60

Herbert McAvoy, Liz (ed.), *A Companion to Julian of Norwich* (Cambridge and Rochester, NY: D.S. Brewer, 2008)

Herbert McAvoy, Liz, 'And Thou to Whom This Book Shall Come: Julian and her Audience, Past, Present and Future', in Dee Dyas et al. (eds.), *Approaching Medieval English Anchoritic and Mystical Texts* (Cambridge: D.S. Brewer, 2005), pp. 101-13

Herbert McAvoy, Liz, *Authority and the Female Body in the Writings of Julian of Norwich and Margery Kemp* (Woodbridge: Boydell Press, 2004)

Herbert McAvoy, Liz, 'Julian and a Trinity of the Feminine', *Mystics Quarterly.* Vol. 28, issue 2 (2002), pp. 68-77

Herbert McAvoy, Liz, 'The Moders Service: Motherhood as Matrix in Julian of Norwich', *Mystics Quarterly.* Vol. 24, issue 4 (December 1998), pp. 181-97

Hide, Kerrie, *Gifted Origins to Graced Fulfillment: The Soteriology of Julian of Norwich* (Collegeville, MN: The Liturgical Press, 2001)

Hide, Kerry, 'Only in God do I Have All: The Soteriology of Julian of Norwich', *Downside Review,* Vol. 122,, issue 426 (January 2004), pp. 43-60

Hide, Kerry, 'The Parable of the Lord and the Servant: A Soteriology for Our Times', *Pacifica,* Vol. 10 (1997), pp. 53-59

Innes-Parker, Catherine, 'Subversion and Conformity in Julian 's Revelation: Authority, Vision and the Motherhood of God', *Mystics Quarterly,* Vol. 23, issue 2 (June 1997), pp. 7-35

Jantzen, Grace, *Becoming Divine: Towards a Feminist Philosophy of Religion* (Bloomington, IN: Indiana University Press, 1999)

Jantzen, Grace, *Julian of Norwich: Mystic and Theologian* (New York and Mahwah, NJ: Paulist Press, 2000)

Jantzen, Grace, *Power, Gender and Christian Mysticism* (Cambridge: Cambridge University Press, 1995)

Johnson, Lynn Staley, 'The Trope of the Scribe and the Question of Literary Authority in the Works of Julian of Norwich and Margery Kemp', *Speculum – A Journal of Medieval Studies,* Vol. 66, issue 4 (1991), pp. 820-38

Lamm, Julia A., 'Revelation as Exposure in Julian of Norwich's Showings', *Spiritus,* Vol. 5, issue 1 (Spring 2005), pp. 54-78

Lang, Judith, 'The Godly Wylle in Julian of Norwich', *Downside Review*, Vol. 162 (1984), pp. 163-72

Liechtmann, Maria R., 'God fulfylled my Bodye: Body, Self and God in Julian of Norwich', in Jane Chance (ed.), *Gender and Text in the Later Middle Ages* (Gainesville, FL: University Press of Florida, 1996)

Liechtmann, Maria R., 'I desyrede a bodylye sight: Julian of Norwich and the Body', *Mystics Quarterly*, Vol. 17, issue 1 (1991), pp. 12-19

Liechtmann, Maria R., 'Julian of Norwich and the Ontology of the Feminine', *Studia Mystica*, Vol. 13, issue 2-3 (1990), pp. 53-65

Llewelyn, Robert, *All Shall Be Well: The Spirituality of Julian of Norwich for Today* (New York: Paulist Press, 1982)

Llewelyn, Robert (ed.), *Julian: Woman of our Day* (London: Darton Longman & Todd, 1985)

Llewelyn, Robert, *With Pity Not with Blame* (London. Darton, Longman & Todd, 1982)

Logarbo, Mona, 'Salvation Theology in Julian of Norwich: Sin, Forgiveness and Redemptions in the *Revelations*', *Thought*, Vol. 61 (1986), pp. 370-380

Magill, Kevin, *Julian of Norwich: Mystic or Visionary* (London and New York: Routledge, 2006)

McEntire, Sandra, *Julian of Norwich: A Book of Essays* (New York: Garland Publishing, 1998)

McEntire, Sandra, 'The Likeness of God and the Restoration of Humanity', in Ann M. Hutchinson (ed.), *Editing Women* (Cardiff: University of Wales Press, 1998), pp. 3-33

McGinn, Bernard, 'The English Mystics', in Jill Raitt (ed.), *Christian Spirituality* (New York: Crossroad, 1987)

McNamer Sarah, 'The Exploratory Image: God as Mother in Julian of Norwich's *Revelations of Divine Love*', *Mystics Quarterly*, Vol. 15., issue 1 (March 1989), pp. 21-28

Norton, Richard, 'Contemplative Prayer and Modern Life; Picture, Ponder Promise: A Parish Retreat with Julian of Norwich', Academia.edu, 2020

Norton, Richard, *How to See a Vision: Contemplative Ethics in Julian of Norwich and Teresa of Avila* (Bloomington, IN: Authorhouse, 2013)

Norton, Richard, *Julian of Norwich and the Doctrine of Salvation* (Eugene, OR: Wipf & Stock, forthcoming)

Norton, Richard, 'Julian of Norwich and Covid 19', Academia edu, 2020

Norton, Richard, *Julian of Norwich: Apostle of Pain* (Bloomington, IN: Authorhouse, 2020)

Norton, Richard, 'Julian's World: Four Themes from the Showings', Academia.edu, 2021

Norton, Richard, 'Praying the Passion with Julian of Norwich: The Stations of the Cross', Academia.edu, 2020

Norton, Richard, 'Themes of Blood, Passion and the *Imitatio Christi* in Julian of Norwich', Academia.edu, 2021

Nuth, Joan M., *God's Lovers in an Age of Anxiety: The English Mystics* (Maryknoll, NY: Orbis Books, 2001)

Nuth, Joan M., 'Two Medieval Soteriologies: Anselm of Canterbury and Julian of Norwich', *Theological Studies*, Vol. 55 (1992), pp. 611-45

Nuth, Joan M., *Wisdom's Daughter: The Theology of Julian of Norwich* (New York: Crossroad, 1991)

Pelphrey, Brant, *Christ Our Mother: Julian of Norwich*. The Way of Christian Mystics Series (Wilmington, DE: Michael Glazier Books, 1989)

Pelphrey, Brant, 'Spirituality in Mission: Lessons from Julian of Norwich', *Cross Currents*, Vol. 34, issue 2 (Summer 1984), pp. 171-90

Pelphrey, Brendan, *Lo How I Love Thee – Divine Love in Julian of Norwich*. Julia Bolton Holloway (ed.) (PLACE?: Spring Deer Studios, 2012)

Peters, Brad, 'Julian of Norwich and her Conceptual Development of Evil', *Mystics Quarterly*, Vol. 17, issue 4 (December 1991), pp. 181-88

Peters, Brad, 'The Reality of Evil within the Mystic Vision of Julian of Norwich', *Mystics Quarterly*, Vol. 13, issue 4 (December 1987), pp. 195-202

Petroff, Elizabeth Alvilda, *Body and Soul: Essays in Medieval Women and Mysticism* (New York and Oxford: Oxford University Press, 1994)

Pinti, Daniel, 'Julian's Audacious Reticence – Perchoresis and The Showing', *Anglican Theological Review*, Vol. 88, issue 4 (2006), pp. 499-517

Reynolds, Anna Maria, 'Courtesy and Homeliness in *Revelation* of Julian of Norwich', *Fourteenth Century English Mystics Newsletter*, Vol. 5 (1978), pp. 12-20

Reynolds, Anna Maria, 'Julian of Norwich: Woman of Hope', *Mystics Quarterly*, Vol. 10, issue 3 (September 1984), pp. 118-25

Reynolds, Anna Maria, 'Woman of Hope', in Robert Llewelyn (ed.), *Julian: Woman of our Day*. (London: Darton Longman & Todd, 1985)

Rudd, Jay Wesley, 'Images of Self and Self Image in Julian of Norwich', *Studia Mystica*, Vol. 1 (1995), pp. 82-108

Sheldrake, Philip, 'A Practical Theology of the Trinity: Julian of Norwich', in *Spirituality and Theology: Christian Living and the Doctrine of God* (Maryknoll, NY: Orbis Books, 1998)

Sheldrake, Philip, *Julian of Norwich in God's Sight: Her Theology in Context* (Chichester: Wiley Blackwell, 2019)

Stately, Lynn, 'Julian of Norwich and the Late Fourteenth Century Crisis of Authority', in David Aers and Lynn Stately (eds.), *The Powers of the Holy: Religion, Politics and Gender in Late Medieval English Culture* (Philadelphia: Pennsylvania University Press, 1996)

Taburr, Karl, 'Mystic Transformation: Julian's Version of the Harrowing of Hell', *Mystics Quarterly*, Vol. 20, issue 2 (1994), pp. 60-67

Turner, Denys, *Julian of Norwich: Theologian* (New Haven, CT: Yale University Press, 2011)

Turner, Denys, 'Sin is Behovenly in Julian of Norwich's *Revelations of Divine Love*', *Modern Theology*, Vol. 20, issue 2 (July 2004), pp. 407-22

Upjohn, Shelia, *In Search of Julian of Norwich* (London: Darton Longman & Todd, 1989)

Upjohn, Shelia, *Why Julian Now? A Voyage of Discovery* (Grand Rapids, MI: William B. Eerdman Publishing Co., 1997)

Watson, Nicholas, 'The Composition of Julian of Norwich's Revelations of Love', *Speculum – A Journal of Medieval Studies,* Vol. 68, issue 3 (1993), pp. 637-83

Watson, Nicholas, 'The Trinitarian Hermeneutics in Julian of Norwich's *Revelations of Love*', in Sandra J. McEntire (ed.), *Julian of Norwich: A Book of Essays* (New York: Garland, 1998), pp. 61-98

Watson, Nicholas, 'Visions and Inclusion – Universal Salvation and Vernacular Theology in Pre-Reformation England', *Journal of Medieval and Early Modern Studies,* Vol. 27, issue 2 (1997), pp. 145-87

Windeatt, Barry, 'Julian of Norwich and her Audience', *Review of English Studies: A Quarterly Journal of English Language and English Literature,* Vol. 28, issue 109 (February 1977), pp. 1-17

Contemporary Debates on the Problem of Evil

Adams, Marilyn McCord, 'Aesthetic Goodness as a Solution to the Problem of Evil', in Sharma Arvind (ed.), *God, Truth and Reality: Essays in Honour of John Hick* (London and New York: Macmillan and St Martin's Press, 1993), pp. 46-61

Adams, Marilyn McCord, '*Chalcedonian Christology: A Christian Solution to the Problem of Evil*', in Stephen T. Davis (ed.), *Philosophy and Theological Discourse* (New York: St Martin's Press, 1997)

Adams, Marilyn McCord, *Christ and Horrors: The Coherence of Christology* (Cambridge: Cambridge University Press, 2006)

Adams, Marilyn McCord, 'Hell and the God of Justice', *Religious Studies,* Vol. 11, issue 4 (December 1975), pp. 433-47

Adams, Marilyn McCord, *Horrendous Evils and the Goodness of God* (Ithaca, NY: Cornell University Press, 1999)

Adams, Marilyn McCord, 'Horrors in Theological Context', *Scottish Journal of Theology,* Vol. 55, issue 4 (2002), pp. 468-79

Adams, Marilyn McCord, 'Problems of Evil: More Advice to Christian Philosophers', *Faith and Philosophy,* Vol. 5, issue 2 (April 1988), pp. 121-43

Adams, Marilyn McCord, 'Redemptive Suffering: A Christian Solution to the Problem of Evil', in Robert Audi and William Wainwright (eds.), *Rationality, Religious Belief and Moral Commitment: New Essays in the Philosophy of Religion* (New York: Cornell University Press, 1986), pp. 248-67

Adams, Marilyn McCord, 'The Coherence of Christology: God Enmattered and Enmattering', *Princeton Seminary Bulletin,* Vol. 26, issue 2 (2005), pp. 157-79

Adams, Marilyn McCord, 'Theodicy without Blame', *Philosophical Topics,* Vol. 16, issue 2 (Fall 1988), pp. 215-45

Adams, Marilyn McCord, 'The Problem of Hell: A Problem of Evil for
    Christians', in Eleanor Stump (ed.), *Reasoned Faith* (Ithaca, NY, and
    London: Cornell University Press, 1992)
Adams, Marilyn McCord and Robert Merrihew (eds.), *The Problem of Evil*
    (Oxford: Oxford University Press, 1990)
Berger, Peter, 'The Problem of Theodicy', in *The Sacred Canopy: Elements of a
    Sociological Theory of Religion* (Garden City, NY: Doubleday & Co., 1967),
    chapter 3
Brock, Rita, *Journeys by Heart: A Christology of Erotic Power* (New York:
    Crossroad, 1988)
Brummer, Vincent, 'Can God Do Evil, Can Theodicy Console?', in *Speaking
    of a Personal God: An Essay in Philosophical Theology* (Cambridge:
    Cambridge University Press, 1992)
Carr, Brian, 'Pity and Compassion as Social Virtues', *Philosophy,* Vol. 74, issue
    289 (July 1999)
Chopp, Rebecca S., *The Praxis of Suffering: An Interpretation of Liberation
    and Political Theology* (Maryknoll, NY: Orbis Books, 1986)
Creel, Richard, *Divine Impassibility: An Essay in Philosophical Theology*
    (Cambridge: Cambridge University Press, 1986)
Crysdale, Cynthia, *Embracing Travail: Retrieving the Cross Today* (New York:
    Continuum, 1999)
Davis, Oliver, *A Theology of Compassion: Metaphysics of Difference and the
    Renewal of Tradition* (Cambridge, MA: William B. Eerdmans, 2001)
Davis, Stephen T. (ed.), *Encountering Evil: Live Options in Theodicy* (Atlanta,
    GA: John Knox Press, 1981)
Davis, Stephen T., 'The Problem of Evil in Recent Philosophy', *Review and
    Expositor,* Vol. 82, issue 4 (Fall 1985), pp. 535-48
Duke, David Nelson and Samuel E. Balentine (eds.), 'Theodicy at the Turn
    of Another Century', *Perspectives in Religious Studies,* Vol. 26, issue 3 (Fall
    1999), pp. 239-360
Farley, Wendy, *Tragic Vision and Divine Compassion: A Contemporary
    Theodicy* (Louisville, KY: Westminster/John Knox Press, 1990)
Fiddes, Paul, *The Creative Suffering of God* (Oxford: Clarendon Press, 1988)
Foyle, Anastasia, 'Human and Divine Suffering: The Relation between
    Human Suffering and the Rise of Passibility Theology', *Ars Disputandi, the
    on-line Journal for Philosophy of Religion,* Vol. 5 (November 2005)
Foyle, Anastasia, 'Review of *Christian Faith and the Problem of Evil*', *Ars
    Disputandi, the on-line Journal for Philosophy of Religion,* Vol. 6 (2006)
Griffin, David, *Evil Revisited: Responses and Reconsiderations* (Albany, NY:
    SUNY Press, 1991)
Griffin, David, *God, Power and Evil* (Philadelphia: Westminster Press, 1976)
Goetz, Ronald, 'The Suffering of God: The Rise of a New Orthodoxy', *The
    Christian Century* (April 1986), pp. 385-38
Hallman, Joseph, *The Descent of God: Divine Suffering in History and
    Theology* (Minneapolis: Fortress Press, 1991)

Hartshorne, Charles, 'A New Look at the Problem of Evil', in F.C. Dommeyer (ed.), *Current Philosophical Issues: Essays in Honour of Curt John Ducasse* (Springfield: C.C. Thomas, 1966), pp. 201-12

Hauerwas, Stanley, *Naming the Silence: Medicine and the Problem of Human Suffering* (Grand Rapids, MI: William B. Eerdmans Publishing Co., 1990)

Herdt, Jennifer, 'The Rise of Sympathy and the Question of Divine Suffering', *Journal of Religious Ethics,* Vol. 29, issue 3 (Fall 2001), pp. 367-99

Hick, John, 'Eschatological Verification Reconsidered', *Religious Studies,* Vol. 13, issue 2 (June 1977), pp. 189-202

Hick, John, *Evil and the God of Love* (London: Fount Paperbacks, Collins, 1979)

Hick, John, 'God, Evil and Mystery', *Religious Studies,* Vol. 3, issue 2 (1968), pp. 539-46

Hick, John, 'The Logic of God Incarnate', *Religious Studies,* Vol. 25, issue 4 (December 1989), pp. 409-23

Hick, John, 'The Problem of Evil', in Paul Edwards (ed.), *Encyclopedia of Philosophy,* Vol. 3 (New York: Macmillan, 1967)

Inbody, Tyron, *The Transforming God: An Interpretation of Suffering and Evil* (Lousville, KY: Westminster/John Knox Press, 1997)

Inwagen, Peter van, *Christian Faith and the Problem of Evil* (Grand Rapids, MI: Eerdmans, 2004)

Keating, James F. and Thomas J. White (eds.), *Divine Impassibility and the Mystery of Human Suffering* (Grand Rapids, MI: Eerdmans, 2009)

Lee, Jung Young, *God Suffers for Us: A Systematic Inquiry into a Concept of Divine Passibility* (The Hague: Martinus Nijhoff, 1974)

Leibniz, G.W., *Theodicy,* tr. E.M. Huggard (London: Routledge, Kegan & Paul, 1951)

Louw, Daniel, '*Fides Quaerens Spem*: A Pastoral and Theological Response to Suffering and Evil', *Interpretation* (October 2003), pp. 384-97

Maudlin, Frank L. 'Misplaced Concreteness in the Problem of Evil', *Perspectives in Religious Studies,* Vol. 11, issue 3 (Fall 1984)

McGill Arthur, *Suffering: A Test of Theological Method* (Philadelphia: Westminster Press, 1982)

McWilliams, Warren, 'A Kenotic God and the Problem of Evil', *Encounter,* Vol. 42, issue 1 (Winter 1981), pp. 15-27

McWilliams, Warren, 'Divine Suffering in Contemporary Theology', *Scottish Journal of Theology,* Vol. 33, issue 1 (1980), pp. 35-53

McWilliams, Warren, 'Only a Triune God Can Help: The Relation of the Trinity to Theodicy', *Perspectives in Religious Studies,* Vol. 33, issue 3 (Fall 2006), pp. 345-59

McWilliams, Warren, *The Passion of God: Divine Suffering in Contemporary Protestant Theology* (Macon, GA: Mercer University Press, 1985)

Moltmann, Jürgen, *The Church in the Power of the Spirit: A Contribution to Messianic Ecclesiology* (London: SCM Press, 1977)

Moltmann, Jürgen, 'The Crucified God', *Theology Today,* Vol. 31, issue 1 (April 1974)

Moltmann, Jürgen, *The Crucified God: The Cross of Christ as Foundation and Criticism of Christian Theology* (London: SCM Press, 2001)

Moltmann, Jürgen, *The Way of Jesus Christ: Christology in Messianic Dimensions* (San Francisco: Harper Press, 1989)

Obiezu, Emeka Christian, *Towards a Politics of Compassion: Socio-Political Dimensions of Christian Responses to Suffering* (Bloomington, IN: AuthorHouse, 2008)

O'Connor, David, 'In Defense of Theoretical Theodicy' *Modern Theology,* Vol. 5 (1988), pp. 61-74

Pinnock, Sarah, *Beyond Theodicy: Jewish and Continental Thinkers Respond to the Holocaust* (Albany, NY: SUNY Press, 2002)

Plantinga, Alvin, *God, Freedom and Evil* (New York. Harper & Row, 1974)

Pope John Paul II, *On the Christian Meaning of Human Suffering* (Boston: St Paul's Books and Media, 1984)

Reynolds, Thomas, *Vulnerable Communion: A Theology of Disability and Hospitality* (New York: Bazos Press, 2008)

Richard, Lucien, *What are they Saying about the Theology of Suffering?* (New York: Paulist Press, 1992)

Roberts, Robert C., 'Compassion', *The Christian Century* (5-12 January 1983)

Sarot, Marcel, 'Divine Suffering: Continuity and Discontinuity with the Tradition', *Anglican Theological Review,* Vol. 78, issue 2 (Spring 1996), pp. 225-40

Sarot, Marcel, 'Patripassianism, Theopaschitism and the Suffering of God: Some Historical and Systematic Considerations', *Religious Studies,* Vol. 26, issue 3 (September 1990), pp. 363-75

Schaab, Gloria L., 'A Procreative Paradigm of the Creative Suffering of the Triune God: Implications of Arthur Peacock's Evolutionary Theology', *Theological Studies,* Vol. 67, issue 3 (September 2006), pp. 542-66

Schaab, Gloria L., *Creative Suffering of the Triune God: An Evolutionary Theology* (Oxford: Oxford University Press, 2007)

Sheldrake, Philip, *Spirituality and Theology: Christian Living and the Doctrine of God* (Maryknoll, NY: Orbis Books, 1998)

Simoni, Henry, 'Divine Passibility and the Problem of Radical Particularity: Does God Feel Your Pain?', *Religious Studies,* Vol. 33, issue 3 (September 1997)

Simpson, Robert, 'Some Moral Critique of Theodicy is Misplaced, But Not All', *Religious Studies,* Vol. 45, issue 3 (September 2009), pp. 339-46

Sölle, Dorothy, *Christ the Representative: An Essay in Theology After the 'Death of God'*, tr. David Lewis (Philadelphia: Westminster Press, 1984)

Sölle, Dorothy, 'God's Plan and our Plan', in Mark Ellis and Otto Maduro (eds.), *The Future of Liberation Theology* (Maryknoll, NY: Orbis Books, 1989)

Sölle, Dorothy, *Suffering,* tr. Everett R. Kahlin (Philadelphia: Fortress Press, 1984)

Sölle, Dorothy, *The Silent Cry: Mysticism and Resistance* (Minneapolis: Fortress Press, 2001)

Sölle, Dorothy, *The Strength of the Weak: Towards a Christian Feminist Identity,* tr. Robert and Rita Kember (Philadelphia: Westminster Press, 1984)

Sölle, Dorothy, *Thinking about God: An Introduction to Theology* (Philadelphia: Trinity Press International, 1990)

Sovik, Atle O., 'Why Almost All Moral Critique of Theodicies is Misplaced', *Religious Studies,* Vol. 44, issue 4 (December 2008), pp. 479-84

Stiver, Dan R., 'The Problem of Theodicy', *Review and Expositor,* Vol. 93, issue 4 (Fall 1996), pp. 507-17

Stoeber, Michael, *Evil and the Mystics: Towards a Mystical Theodicy* (Toronto: University of Toronto Press, 1992)

Stoeber, Michael, *Reclaiming Theodicy: Reflections on Suffering, Compassion and Spiritual Transformation* (New York and Houndmills: Palgrave Macmillan, 2005)

Stoeber, Michael, 'Transformative Suffering, Destructive Suffering and the Question of Spiritual Transformation', *Studies in Religion,* Vol. 32, issue 4 (2003), pp. 429-47

Suchoki, Marjorie, *The End of Evil: Process Eschatology in Historical Context* (Albany, NY: SUNY Press, 1988)

Suchoki, Marjorie, *The Fall of Violence: Original Sin in Theological Perspective* (New York: Continuum International Publishing Group, 1994)

Surin, Kenneth, 'Terrence Tilley's *The Evils of Theodicy*', *Horizons,* Vol. 18, issue 2 (Fall 1991), pp. 290-306

Surin, Kenneth, *Theology and the Problem of Evil* (Oxford: Blackwells, 1986)

Surin, Kenneth, 'Theodicy?', *Harvard Theological Review,* 76 (1983), pp. 225-47

Surin, Kenneth, 'The Impassibility of God and the Problem of Evil', *Scottish Journal of Theology,* 35 (1982), pp. 97–115

Swinburne, Richard, *Providence and the Problem of Evil* (New York: Oxford University Press, 1988)

Swinton, John, *Raging with Compassion: Pastoral Response to the Problem of Evil* (Grand Rapids, MI: William B. Eerdmans, 2007)

Taliaferro, Charles, 'The Passibility of God', *Religious Studies,* Vol. 25, issue 2 (June 1989), pp. 217–24

Tilley, Terrence, *The Evils of Theodicy* (Washington, DC: Georgetown University Press, 1991)

Tilley, Terrence, 'The Use and Abuse of Theodicy', *Horizons,* Vol. 11 (1984), pp. 304–19

Weil, Simone, 'The Love of God and Affliction', in *Simone Weil Writings,* ed. Eric O. Springsted (Maryknoll, NY: Orbis Books, 1998)

Weinandy, Thomas, *Does God Suffer?* (Notre Dame, IN: University of Notre Dame, 2000)

Weinandy, Thomas, 'Does God Suffer?', *First Things*, Vol. 117 (November 2001), pp. 35–41

Whitney, Barry L., *Theodicy: An Annotated Bibliography on the Problem of Evil. 1960–1991* (Bowling Green, OH: Bowling Green State University Press, 1998)

Whitney, Barry L., *What are they Saying about Good and Evil?* (Mahwah, NJ: Paulist Press, 1989)

Index

Printed and bound by CPI Group (UK) Ltd, Croydon, CR0 4YY